The Mediterranean Herb Cookbook

THE
MEDITERRANEAN HERB
COOKBOOK

Fresh and Savory Recipes from the Mediterranean Garden

GEORGEANNE BRENNAN

PHOTOGRAPHS BY GREY CRAWFORD

CHRONICLE BOOKS
SAN FRANCISCO

Library of Congress Cataloging-in-Publication Data:

The Mediterranean herb cookbook: fresh and savory recipes from the Mediterranean garden / by Georgeanne Brennan: photographs by Grey Crawford.

    p. cm.

    ISBN 0-8118-1990-6

    1. Cookery (Herbs) 2. Herbs. 3. Cookery, Mediterranean.

    I. Title

    TX819.H4B6985   2000

    641.6'57—dc21   99-40462

                    CIP

Printed in Hong Kong.

Styling by Ethel Brennan

Props by Carol Hacker

Photography assistance by Kristen Loken

Design by Pamela Geismar

Background image throughout book
    copyright © Hans Silvester – Rapho

Distributed in Canada by Raincoast Books

8680 Cambie Street

Vancouver, British Columbia V6P 6M9

10 9 8 7 6 5 4 3 2 1

Chronicle Books

85 Second Street

San Francisco, California 94105

www.chroniclebooks.com

ACKNOWLEDGMENTS

I would especially like to thank Charlotte Kimball, my former partner in the seed business, for teaching me so much about herbs. I would also like to thank the people at Oldways for making a research trip to Crete possible, and the International Olive Oil Council and Foodcom, Inc. for making possible research trips to Tunisia, Spain, and Sicily. Over the years the staff at the University of California at Davis has been very helpful in sharing and making available herbal research and information. I would also like to thank Paula Wolfert for sharing her vast knowledge of Mediterranean herbs, and Georgina Fine and Marie Palazolli for teaching me to gather the wild herbs and greens of Provence. Thanks to my husband, Jim Schrupp, for growing so many herbs for me, for loving food cooked with herbs as much as I do, and for being the very best partner I could have. Many thanks to my children Ethel and Oliver Brennan, Tom and Dan Schrupp for being such enthusiasts about cooking with herbs, and for carrying on the tradition in their own lives. And, a very special thank you to Ethel, who is not only my daughter but also a talented and perceptive food stylist whose beautiful work is apparent throughout this book. Thank you to Bill LeBlond, my editor at Chronicle Books, and his assistant Stephanie Rosenbaum, for seeing this book through its various changes, and to Pamela Geismar for taking the design in hand, as well as to Grey Crawford and his assistant Kristen Loken for the inspired natural-light photography. A very special thank you to my copy editor, Sharon Silva, who helped me shape this book during its development.

Contents

INTRODUCTION 9

Using Culinary Herbs 13

Small Dishes, Salads, and Soups 29

Main Courses 61

Breads and Sweets 87

Basic Herbal Recipes 107

Growing Your Own Herbs 137

BIBLIOGRAPHY 149

INDEX 150

TABLE OF EQUIVALENTS 156

INTRODUCTION

Herbs are an essential ingredient in the Mediterranean diet, an uncomplicated regimen built primarily on vegetables, fruits, grains, fish, and olive oil. Despite such simplicity, it is some of the world's best-tasting food. Indeed, it is not surprising that people are captivated, seduced even, by the fragrantly herbed foods of Italy and Provence, of Spain and Greece. A platter of local cucumbers—sliced into thick rounds, sprinkled with red onion, drizzled with deep green olive oil, and strewn with aromatic mint or basil—served up in a Greek café, a Spanish bodega, or an Italian trattoria is memorable. A rockfish stuffed with branches of dried fennel and seasoned with thyme, salt, and pepper exudes a richness of flavor that belies its simplicity. Fortunately, the Mediterranean table is easy to emulate no matter where you live. Its style is uncomplicated and its rules are few: the freshest of ingredients, red meat introduced sparingly, and olive oil and fresh herbs used profusely.

Although the specific herbs vary from country to country and region to region, the Mediterranean style of cooking employs herbs throughout. In Turkey and Greece, dill is more commonly used than it is in southern France or Spain, while thyme permeates the cooking of southern France and Italy.

The North African countries rely heavily on cilantro, parsley, and mint, which are also used with a free hand in Lebanon, Turkey, and Greece. Oregano, both fresh and dried, is especially popular in Spain, Italy, Greece, and Turkey, but all the countries use it to some degree.

Because Mediterranean cooking is generally simple—grilling, soups, stews, fresh salads—the herbs that grow so readily in the region play an important role in flavoring. Using herbs, especially fresh herbs, in abundance means that even the most humble foods—steamed potatoes, freshly grated carrots, springtime's first peas, pasta tossed with greens, braised white beans—need only a sprinkling of chopped fresh thyme, or perhaps fennel or parsley, to complement their tastes and make them soar. The herbs are singularly important because the flavors, and thus the pleasure and satisfaction derived from a meal, come primarily from them rather than from flavor-rich meat fat or elaborate butter-based sauces. Through their volatile oils, herbs engage our senses of smell and taste, which heighten both the anticipation of the food and its enjoyment. Before we sample a plate of tomatoes strewn with fresh basil, the beckoning aroma of the basil prepares our palate for the taste to come, as does a cup of hot tea infused with the fragrance of fresh mint, or a bowl of pasta-laced broth issuing the scent of thyme and rosemary.

The Mediterranean basin is home to the majority of the most popular culinary herbs, including bay, thyme, rosemary, sage, marjoram, oregano, parsley, fennel, and mint, as well as the less familiar celery-flavored lovage and licorice-like sweet cicely. The cooking found in the countries that ring the Mediterranean Sea has long been characterized by the use of these herbs and the indigenous fish, fruits, and vegetables. Centuries of trading with Arabia, Africa, and later the New World and the Far East introduced other herbs, such as basil, nasturtium, and tarragon. They arrived along with a number of new vegetables—tomatoes, eggplants, beans, peppers—and were soon flourishing in their new environment.

Although each of the Mediterranean countries and, indeed, each region within those countries, has a distinct cuisine shaped by geography, conflicts, religion, and trading, they all share an approach to cooking that can be called Mediterranean and that incorporates one or more herbs in almost every savory dish. This book, however, is not meant to be a reportage or collection of authentic Mediterranean dishes, as there are many other excellent books that accomplish that. Instead, the recipes and the culinary ideas found here are inspired by the Mediterranean style of cooking, and they reflect our

own taste and our own often busy schedules that have little room for devoting long hours to complex preparations. A grilled fish, brushed with olive oil, might be seasoned with rosemary, fennel, thyme, or cilantro and mint. The dish isn't specific to any one place or country, but it still expresses the Mediterranean style of cooking. The purpose of this book is twofold: to draw upon the long-established Mediterranean cooking tradition that relies upon herbs for flavoring the simple—and best—ingredients and to act as a handbook for people who want to grow their own herbs.

As an unabashed lover of herbs and a passionate believer of their importance in the kitchen, I want to encourage everyone to grow even a few herbs so that they might enjoy the pleasure of using fresh herbs in everyday cooking. It is surprising how clipping two or three sprigs of basil from a windowsill pot can transform even a frozen pizza or a basic pasta dish. Many people balk at the notion of growing herbs, feeling that they have a black thumb or not enough time or skill to cultivate them, but many herbs are easily and quickly grown from seed, including arugula, dill, cilantro, and borage. Seedlings both of annuals like basil, chives, and summer savory and perennials such as rosemary, thyme, sage, and mint are readily available at nurseries. All you have to do is bring them home and put them in a pot or in the ground. Even if you find your green thumb is slow to develop, you will discover enormous satisfaction from buying pots of chives, parsley, and rosemary and snipping leaves from them over several weeks. Should they eventually fail under your care, the return on your investment will have been enough to encourage you to replace them and continue to cook with fresh herbs as your green thumb develops. Thus, while this book is primarily a cookbook with light, quick, and easy Mediterranean-inspired recipes to suit today's busy lifestyles, it is also a gardening book.

The book consists of four main parts. The first introduces twenty-seven different culinary herbs, divided into two groups, green and woody. Each entry details different varieties, culinary uses, and traditions. These entries are preceded by a brief description of the importance of herbs in the Mediterranean kitchen.

The second part is made up of recipes divided into three chapters: Small Dishes, Salads, and Soups; Main Courses; and Breads and Sweets. The third part presents an extensive recipe glossary for basic herbal preparations: sauces, marinades, butters, herb blends, oils, vinegars, and beverages, as well as suggestions on how to use and serve them. The final section offers information on selecting, preparing, and maintaining a site or containers for a small herb garden, along with information on growing the twenty-seven different culinary herbs discussed in part one.

It is my wish that this book will inspire people to grow fresh herbs, to cook with them with confidence, and to share with me the pleasure of participating in the natural world in this small, but delicious, way.

Using Culinary Herbs

Culinary herbs are plants, either wild or cultivated, that provide flavoring for food. They are used both fresh and dried as a secondary ingredient in cooking, although some herbs, such as parsley, cilantro, young fennel, and dandelion, also act as primary ingredients. The leaves, buds, and blossoms of fresh herbs are used culinarily, while the seeds of some herbs—dill, fennel, cilantro—are typically used dried as spices, serving a dual role in the kitchen.

Herbs activate our senses—visual, tactile, olfactory, and, above all, gustatory. When fresh, the oils that create their characteristic flavors are at their most intense, and the fragrance and taste they bring to the table have no equal.

Two distinct types exist: delicate, short-lived, green herbs like chervil and tarragon, which are quite fragile and bruise easily, and sturdy, long-lasting woody herbs such as thyme and rosemary. All of them can be used either fresh or dried, but many of the green herbs lose their flavor and intensity when dried, so they are best used fresh. Other herbs, especially the woody ones, retain their fragrance and flavor after drying.

To the people who live around the Mediterranean basin, daily cooking with herbs is second nature. Even today, when modern life has transformed many Mediterranean seaside cities and once-quiet fishing villages into bustling international metropolises, and interior plains and valleys into suburbs and high-rise industrial parks, the traditional use of herbs continues to play an important culinary role.

Vendors in the open markets of Spain, France, Italy, Cypress, Yugoslavia, Croatia, Turkey, Israel, Lebanon, Egypt, Libya, Tunisia, Morocco, and Algeria sell herbs, both fresh and dried, all year long. In the market stalls, stacks of fresh rosemary, bay leaves, blue-flowered borage, and leafy fennel stalks are arranged side by side with bags heaped full of aromatic dried thyme, oregano, and mint, their fragrance drawing passersby inward. In produce markets and supermarkets in the most cosmopolitan areas, residents can readily find local fresh and dried herbs.

Collecting wild herbs in the countryside is still a customary pastime in the Mediterranean, where knowledge of which herbs to pick and the best time of year to gather them has been passed down through the generations. Nearly any time of the year it is possible to see representatives from three generations walking the hillsides or edges of the fields, baskets on their arms, harvesting the seasonal herbs. In Crete, where wild herbs and greens are an essential part of culinary tradition, March and April find the hillsides lush with thickets of young fennel, borage, and sorrel. They are carried away by the armloads and used to stuff savory pies and flavor soups, stews, and salads. In southern France, late May, when the wild thyme is abloom with purple flowers, is a prime moment to snip this important regional herb, and the smallest of children are able to distinguish it by its blossoms and fragrance. Later, in summer, it will be time to gather the wild oregano called marjorlaine. In spring and fall, dandelion, sorrel, and fennel are collected, along with wild mushrooms and asparagus.

Although a number of the most common culinary herbs grow wild in the United States, most of us lack the knowledge to be able to identify them, with perhaps the exception of fennel, mint, and dandelion. Consequently, most herbs are commercially grown or raised in home gardens. Generally, those that are cultivated tend to have a slightly milder flavor than those in the wild. This is because they are irrigated, that is, given a steady supply of water, and thus their volatile oils are more diluted. Thus, to achieve the flavor you want, you may need to use more of a cultivated herb than you do of a wild one. I know that when I am cooking in France with the wild herbs I gather there, I use them more sparingly than I do the herbs that I grow at home in California.

Certainly fresh and dried herbs are available in our supermarkets and farmers' markets, but there is nothing quite like stepping out your kitchen door to cut them fresh from the garden and add them directly to whatever you are cooking. When you have grown and dried your own herbs, you know their age and can use them with confidence. This is important because dried herbs begin to lose their flavor and may begin to taste a little stale and dusty after six months.

⌘

Green Herbs

Green herbs are those that generally have a high water content and consequently are not long-lived once cut. For the most part, they are used fresh because much of their flavor and aroma are lost when dried. In the garden they have a greater need for water than do the woody herbs, and thus care must be taken if the two types are planted together, as the woody ones can suffer from overwatering and the green from underwatering. The seeds of angelica, cilantro, dill, and fennel are also used for cooking, and so these plants play the dual role of herb and spice. In addition, their blossoms, like those of all the green herbs, are edible.

Many of the green herbs are delicate and their flavor can rapidly dissipate when cooked. To ensure maximum effect, it is generally best to add them toward the end of cooking or just before serving. All the green herbs are outstanding in salads as flavoring agents, and many of them, such as chervil, tarragon, cilantro, sorrel, and dill, can be used more boldly as major elements. The storage life of most is brief, and their texture, appearance, and flavor deteriorate quickly, so whenever possible use green herbs shortly after harvest. If you are choosing them at a farmers' market or in the produce department, they should have no signs of yellowing or slipperiness on the leaves and stems, an indication of aging, and the leaves should be free of black spots, which are a sign of damage from cold weather or improper refrigeration after harvest. A handful of the green herbs are candidates for drying. Directions on how to dry them appear on page 21.

ANGELICA *(Angelica archangelica)* Biennial
Sweet-smelling angelica is used primarily as a confectionery decoration, in the form of its candied stems. It also serves to reduce the tartness of acidic fruits like rhubarb and plums. The stems toughen as the plant matures, so they should be cut when young and candied right away. They are particularly popular in Sicily, southern Spain, and southwestern France, where there is a tradition of carving them into varied shapes. Although its culinary use is not widespread, angelica is a lovely, showy addition to a Mediterranean-inspired herb garden.

ARUGULA *(Eruca sativa)*
Also called rocket, arugula is a popular wild and cultivated herb in the Mediterranean, especially in Italy and southern France where it is considered an indispensable ingredient in salad mixtures of green herbs and lettuces. The young, tender leaves taste faintly nutty, but as they mature they become quite large, distinctly peppery, and coarse, and snippets, rather than whole leaves, are used fresh. Whole mature leaves can be cooked and treated as a green, much like spinach or chard. Wild arugula, a different strain, has thinner leaves and an intense peppery flavor attenuated by a distinct sweetness. It can overwhelm other flavors, so it is best used sparingly.

In Italian households, arugula is combined with ricotta and Parmesan and used to stuff manicotti, cannelloni, or other pasta, and is also tossed with pasta as part of a sauce. It combines well with citrus or tomatoes in salads, where its sharp flavor contrasts nicely with the sweet acidity of the fruits.

Once arugula is cut, sprinkle it with a little water, put it in a plastic bag, and store in the crisper of the refrigerator, where it will keep for several days.

BASIL *(Ocimum basilicum)*
There are numerous types of basil, all of which are typically used fresh because dried basil loses much of its distinctively spiced, perfumed, and sometimes slightly peppery flavor. A salad of tomatoes, fresh mozzarella, and basil is a classic Italian combination, while in the eastern Mediterranean basil is minced with tarragon and mint or chives to make a topping for yogurt, vegetables, and meats. When using it in cooked dishes, such as soups, sauces, or as a garnish for vegetables, add it at the last minute, as rapid heating dissipates the flavor. Oil or vinegar infused with basil can be made ahead and stored and then used to flavor other dishes.

Once harvested, basil's life is short. It is very sensitive to cold, so even the standard home refrigerator can cause damage. To protect basil in the refrigerator, wrap it in damp paper towels, then put it in a plastic bag in the crisper, where it will keep for two or three days. It can also be kept in a glass or jar of water, like a bouquet of flowers, for four or five days on a windowsill. Ideally, use it within a short time of purchase or straight from the garden.

BORAGE *(Borago officinalis)*
Although today fresh borage is one of the lesser-known herbs, it has been used for centuries as both an herb and a potherb, or kitchen green. Its most distinctive characteristic is its bright blue, star-shaped flowers, which make wonderful sugared candies for decorating cakes or other sweets and for adding to drinks such as lemonade or limeade. The young, tender leaves have a faint cucumber flavor that goes well in salads, soups, and pasta dishes. When used in quantity, the leaves and stems can be cooked like spinach or other greens and then served as a side dish or combined with other ingredients to stuff pasta or crepes. In Sicily and Crete, borage is gathered in the wild and sold in the markets.

The leaves have an initially daunting furry covering, especially the larger ones, but this disappears after cooking. Borage is not often marketed in the United States as a fresh herb, so storage is rarely an issue. Since the herb is so easy and beautiful to grow, however, you can keep a plant or two growing in your garden, using the leaves, stems, and flowers as you snip them.

CHERVIL (*Anthriscus cerefolium*)

Chervil, along with chives, tarragon, and parsley, is one of the *fines herbes* of classic French cooking. They are all quite fragile and are best used either raw or added to a cooked dish only at the last minute. When dried, chervil loses its character, and it then contributes little else to a dish than its bright green color.

Its lemon-anise flavor and crisp texture make chervil a prized ingredient in parts of southern France and northern Italy, where it is considered an essential element in the regional salad mixtures, *mesclun* and *misticanza* respectively. It is also frequently used in fish and egg dishes and in delicate sauces.

To protect harvested chervil, wrap it in damp paper towels and put it in a plastic bag in the crisper of the refrigerator, or omit the paper towels and instead sprinkle the chervil lightly with water, then store it in a plastic bag. In either case, use the chervil within two or three days, as it deteriorates rapidly.

CHIVE (*Allium schoenoprasum*)

Chives are culinarily noteworthy members of the onion family because of the subtle but sharp flavor they bring to a dish. Their buds, and the lavender-colored blossoms that appear in late spring and early summer, have a mild onion taste that also can be used in cooking. As one of the *fines herbes*, chives are used uncooked to flavor butters, cheeses, and vinaigrettes. They are a common addition to egg and chicken dishes and to steamed vegetables of all kinds. They form a component in the mixtures of fresh green herbs that have found their way to the tables of the eastern Mediterranean by way of Arabia and are sprinkled into soups, stews, and atop vegetable dishes, often accompanied with yogurt.

Another variety of chives, called garlic chives (*A. tuberosum*), may also be cultivated for the home herb garden, although seeds and plants may be more difficult to find than those of common chives. Garlic chives are grown from bulbs and have flat, as opposed to tubular, stems, which are often blanched (protected from sunlight) to keep them pale yellow and mild tasting. Their flavor, as the name indicates, is slightly garlicky. They are used primarily in Asian cooking, although they may be used in the same way as common chives.

Once cut, chives will last several days in the refrigerator, either in plastic bags or wrapped in paper towels. They can also be kept in a glass or jar of water on the windowsill for a day or two. Better yet, keep a pot of chives growing on a kitchen windowsill or other light-filled location, to provide fresh snips as needed.

CILANTRO (*Coriandrum sativum*)

Also known as coriander and Chinese parsley, cilantro is one of the herbs whose seeds, referred to as coriander, are also used for flavoring. The term *fresh coriander* is used to distinguish it from the seeds. The leaves, flowers, and roots are especially pungent and are used fresh, while the seeds are far more commonly used dried. Fresh cilantro has a rich, slightly perfumed flavor, and the dried seeds are aromatic and spicy.

Cilantro is amenable to both sweets and savories, and is as much at home in a fresh fruit salad as it is in a potato salad. In the eastern Mediterranean and North Africa, it is often used in combination with other green herbs to make a refreshing condiment for spiced dishes, and it is frequently partnered with yogurt or lemon juice. In Tunisian and Moroccan cooking cilantro is used by the handfuls. It is prominent in the local markets, where it is sold in big bunches. It makes an excellent addition to soups and sauces, especially those with a tomato base. Although native to the Mediterranean, cilantro has come to be more closely linked with the cuisines of Mexico, Southeast Asia, and India, where it is used extensively. As with other delicate green herbs, the leaves lose much of their potency when dried, and are best used fresh, added at the end of cooking.

Cilantro deteriorates rapidly after being harvested. Even when it is carefully stored in damp paper towels inside a plastic bag, it can become slimy after a few days. Like basil, it is also sensitive to chilling, causing the leaf tissue to die and turn black.

DANDELION *(Taraxacum officinale)*

Most often treated as a salad green, dandelion grows wild throughout the Mediterranean. It is collected for its tart green leaves and for its root, which has a fine, much appreciated bitter flavor. Like many of the green herbs, it is typically used fresh, not dried. Snippets of the leaves add a sprightly flavor to soups and to vegetable salads made of potatoes, carrots, beets, or beans.

In green salads, the leaves of wild dandelion are often served on their own in a classic combination of eggs, bacon, and onions, or mixed with other strong-flavored greens such as beet tops, arugula, and frisée and dressed with a garlic vinaigrette. For a milder presentation, you can toss a few leaves into a salad of butter lettuce.

In French markets, cultivated dandelion greens, varieties such as 'Dandelion de Montmargny' are commonly available, but I have rarely found them outside of France. Occasionally, I do find greens labeled dandelion in California, but they are actually a chicory, either 'San Pasquale' or 'Catalonia,' and the leaves are considerably larger, thicker, and deeper green

and have more substantial midribs than either wild or cultivated dandelion. Like chard, these greens are better cooked than served in a salad because they are rather fibrous and quite strong flavored. The roots are scraped clean, then minced and added to salads or to the salad dressing.

Once dandelion is cut, sprinkle it with water and store it in a plastic bag in the crisper of the refrigerator. Leave the root unpeeled until you are ready to use it, then trim off root hairs and tough brownish skin by scraping with a sharp knife or with a vegetable peeler.

DILL *(Anethum graveolens)*

Although dill is a Mediterranean native that features heavily in Scandinavian and northern and eastern European cooking, it can be found growing wild in the United States in the middle of the Atlantic seaboard. It is also used extensively in the cooking of Turkey and Greece in such dishes as carrot soup, eggplant purée, and tomato and feta salads. It is one of the most popular of the green herbs, prized for both its seeds and leaves. The large, airy seed heads, abloom with tiny yellow flowers, are an essential pickling ingredient. They are cut when some of the seeds have begun to ripen and used whole as a pickling spice. The leaves lose a lot of flavor during cooking or drying, so they are best used fresh or, if dried, in volume.

Fresh dill can be added at the end of cooking or used as a raw garnish. The leaves go well with mild foods like cheeses, omelets, salads, and seafoods. Dill seed is used in such slow-cooked dishes as meat stews and braised vegetables, especially cabbage and root vegetables. The herb retains its flavor when dried.

Store fresh dill in a plastic bag in the crisper of the refrigerator for several days.

FENNEL *(Foeniculum vulgare)*

Fennel is one of the most prevalent of wild herbs in the Mediterranean basin, where its leaves, stems, and seeds are used with abandon. Its pollen is collected in Italy and used for its mild flavor to season fish and pasta dishes, among others. It also grows wild along the roadsides and in the small towns and meadows of California, the Pacific Northwest, the eastern seaboard, and Louisiana, areas of the United States with temperate climates comparable to that of the Mediterranean. Cultivated fennel, grown in home herb gardens and by commercial growers, has the same licorice flavor as wild fennel, but it is milder, as is the flavor of its seeds and stems. Florence fennel, of which there are numerous varieties, is a strain that was developed for its bulbous base, which is used as a vegetable, although its leaves, stems, and seeds are used for seasoning as well.

When fish are stuffed with fennel stems and leaves and then grilled, the herb's aroma gently infuses the flesh. Fresh fennel is used to flavor soups, salads, and sauces and in mixtures with other green herbs to create fresh herb blends. In areas of the eastern Mediterranean, fennel leaves gathered in bunches are treated like greens and simmered with olive oil and vegetables or meats. In southern France, Spain, and Greece, the stalks are used to add flavoring during cooking, then removed before serving. The seeds are deeply aromatic and can be used whole or crushed in sweets and breads and as an element in marinades.

Fennel greens wilt quickly. Wrap them in moist paper towels and store in plastic bags in the crisper of the refrigerator, where they will keep two or three days. Spread freshly harvested seeds in a single layer on a baking sheet or tray and leave to dry in a nonhumid area for a day or two, then store in a closed container.

LEMON VERBENA
(Aloysia triphylla, also called *Lippia citriodora)*

The narrow, apple-green leaves and the lilac-white or whitish blossoms of this handsome plant have a distinctive and pleasing lemon fragrance. The leaves, both fresh and dried, are used to flavor desserts, creams, beverages, and fruit dishes. They should be used with discretion, however, as they can be quite potent. Lemon verbena is naturalized throughout the Mediterranean region today, but its origins are in the New World. It is especially popular dried and used for making infusions in southern France and in Tunisia and other North African countries.

Wrap fresh lemon verbena in damp paper towels and store in the crisper of the refrigerator for up to a week. It is also quite flavorful dried.

LOVAGE *(Levisticum officinale)*

Lovage, a native of southern Europe, resembles celery in appearance and flavor but grows quite a bit taller, up to six feet. It is used in much the same way as celery, but its flavor is stronger and can overpower a dish if not used sparingly.

The tender, young leaves that mark the first flush of growth can be added to salads, but older leaves should be confined to slow-cooking soups and stews. The seeds are delicious sprinkled onto salads or other dishes as a garnish. Tunisian cooks sometimes add chopped leaves to fish dishes at the end of cooking. Dried leaves are a good flavoring and are commonly found in herbal tea mixtures.

Store fresh lovage in a plastic bag in the crisper of the refrigerator. It will keep for four or five days.

MINT *(Mentha species)*

Mint is one of the most important herbs in the North African pantry, where it is used in great abundance for making mint tea. Fresh and dried mint are also used in Greece, Turkey, Lebanon, Tunisia, and other countries of the Mediterranean in any number of savory ways to flavor soups, stews, salads, and sauces. One of the most popular sauces, used as a condiment for dipping breads, is a simple one of yogurt, chopped fresh mint, garlic, salt, and pepper. The leaves, whole or chopped, are frequently added to salads made with grains, greens, or vegetables such as peppers, cucumbers, or tomatoes. Mint is one of the green herbs that retains its flavor when dried, although it is more aromatic when fresh. Store fresh mint in a plastic bag in the crisper of the refrigerator where it will keep for three or four days.

NASTURTIUM (*Tropaeolum* species)

There are several nasturtium species, all with the same peppery flavor. In the right climate—slightly cool, slightly moist—they can grow rampantly over a wide area. Both the large, round leaves and the flowers are succulent and can be added freely to green salads, where they will add a piquant note, and the immature green seeds can be pickled in the same manner as capers. The flowers, whole or chopped, are added to salads, butters, or omelets, where they will contribute the same flavor plus their strikingly showy colors. The leaves are used as a green in southern France and in Italy.

The nasturtium is related to watercress, so keep it fairly damp when storing, preferably in a plastic bag along with a wet paper towel in the crisper of the refrigerator. The leaves and blossoms will keep two to three days.

PARSLEY (*Petroselinum crispum*)

Another Mediterranean native, parsley is probably the best known of all the culinary herbs. It is used abundantly throughout the region in many, many dishes. The main varieties are plain or flat leaf, curly leaf, moss leaf, and fern leaf. The curly leaf is the predominant variety in the United States, but the flat leaf, sometimes called Italian parsley, is more popular in Europe, North Africa, and the near East because of its stronger flavor. Parsley is used as a garnish for vegetables and salads, and as a main ingredient in salads, stews, and omelets. It is often used in great quantity when treated as a primary ingredient, especially in Tunisia, Turkey, and Morocco. The flat-leaf type holds up well in long cooking, slowly imparting its rich flavor. The curly leaf is better chopped finely and added as a colorful garnish at the end of cooking. Parsley is an essential ingredient in the classic French *persillade* (page 127) and bouquet garni (page 125) and in Italian *gremolata* (page 127).

Fresh parsley stores well. Slip it into a plastic bag in the crisper of the refrigerator for a week or more, or put it in a glass of water in the refrigerator or on a windowsill out of direct sunlight. If some of the sprigs turn yellow or become slimy, discard them and rinse the rest.

SORREL (*Rumex acetosa*)

The name *sorrel* comes from the word for sour in Old High German, and it is an apt description. The leaves are lance-shaped like spinach and are a similar bright green, but they are high in acid and will discolor when cut unless a stainless steel knife is used. The smaller-leaved French variety, *Rumex scutatus*, is a little milder but also far less available. The new leaves start out mild and get stronger tasting as they age, but constant cutting will provide continued new growth throughout the spring and summer. Sorrel is used in salads, many cream sauces, and especially in the two French favorites, sorrel soup and salmon in sorrel sauce.

You can put fresh sorrel in a plastic bag in the crisper of the refrigerator, but after a day or two the edges of the leaves will start to deteriorate. Snip it and use it the same day if possible.

SUMMER SAVORY (*Satureja hortensis*)

Because they are used to flavor pulses—peas, beans, and lentils, all seeds of the legume family—both the savories, summer and winter, are often called the bean herb. Summer savory is milder in flavor and very easy to grow. It is a Mediterranean native, but has now naturalized over the center of the United States, especially in drier areas. The plant is highly aromatic, somewhat like thyme, and is often used fresh or dried in herb mixtures, for stews, and on chicken or other meats before grilling. Turkish cooking often calls for it, as does the cooking of southern France.

Store fresh summer savory for several days in a plastic bag in the crisper of the refrigerator, in a glass of water kept in the refrigerator, or on a windowsill out of direct sunlight. Summer savory is also quite flavorful dried.

SWEET CICELY (*Myrrhis odorata*) Perennial

Sweet cicely has an anise or fennel flavor combined with a slight celery taste. It is cooked in combination with other greens such as spinach or chard and contributes just a hint of sweetness. The young, tender, somewhat lacy leaves can be added to fruit, vegetable, or green salads, and they are also used to flavor ice creams, poached fruit, and tarts. The seeds are used in sweets and pastries, much like the seeds of anise or fennel.

Store fresh sweet cicely in a plastic bag in the crisper of the refrigerator for two or three days.

TARRAGON (*Artemisia dracunculus*) Perennial

Originally from southern Russia, tarragon grows easily in the Mediterranean basin. The small, shrublike plant has wooden basal branches that produce hundreds of long, green, leaf-lined sprouts that are originally succulent, but get wiry over time. The leaves have a clean, pleasing aroma and a cleansing, licoricelike flavor. The herb is essential in béarnaise and hollandaise sauces and is a powerful addition to butters, mayonnaise, infused vinegars, and especially salads. It is used as a component in mixed green herb blends, along with cilantro, parsley, and dill, often in conjunction with yogurt, especially in the Levant. Be forewarned, though, that it's French tarragon you want, which is grown only from cuttings, and not the inferior, harsh-tasting Russian tarragon, which can be grown from seed.

Dried tarragon leaves retain some of their essential oils. Store fresh in a plastic bag in the crisper of the refrigerator for several days.

DRYING GREEN HERBS

Among the green herbs, lemon verbena, mint, summer savory, and tarragon are worth drying because they retain a goodly portion of their flavor. Since arugula, basil, chervil, chives, cilantro, dill, parsley, and sorrel retain little flavor when dried, and because they are available nearly year-round in farmers' markets and many produce sections, I advise buying them fresh when your own herb garden isn't providing them. To dry green herbs, loosely gather a single variety into a bundle. Tie it with a length of kitchen string and hang it in a warm, dry place with good air circulation. Once dried, the leaves can be trimmed and stored in an airtight container.

The green herbs that are not readily available commercially, including angelica, borage, lovage, and nasturtium, are also those that are best used in season, fresh from the garden, and contribute little to a dish when dried. Basil, chervil, chives, dill, and tarragon can be blanched and then frozen in ice-cube trays where they will retain some of their essence, but since they are usually available fresh, it seems preferable to use them fresh.

Woody Herbs

Woody herbs, all perennials, are usually hardy plants with leaves, blossoms, and woody stems that contain their essential oils. Because of their relatively high content of volatile oils, they are extremely aromatic and retain more of their flavor and aroma when dried than most green herbs do. In a garden setting, the woody herbs tend to require far less water than the green herbs, and, in fact, overwatering can kill sage and rosemary. Typically they are not mixed with green herbs in the garden or containers because of these different water needs. It is important that all these herbs be planted where they will have good drainage.

Of the woody herbs, only lavender and rosemary play the double role of herb and spice. Lavender's blossoms are more frequently used as a flavoring than its leaves, stems, or seeds. The long, woody stems of rosemary and bay are used as skewers for grilling, and branches of all the woody herbs can be added to wood or charcoal grills to infuse the food with their smoky scent.

The woody herbs are much sturdier than their green counterparts, and their flavors are more pungent and longer lasting even when dried. In their fresh form they can be added during any stage of the cooking, even at the beginning of slow roasts and bakes, because they tend to release their essence over time. A fresh bay leaf in a casserole of potatoes baked slowly with milk and onions will suffuse the final dish with its subtle aroma and faintly sweet, woodsy taste. A red wine marinade for lamb shanks with sprigs of fresh thyme and rosemary will impregnate the meat with a resinous taste, distinct but diffused, during a long, slow cooking. Fresh woody herbs can be added at the end of cooking as well, like the traditional topping of minced fresh oregano given to pizzas emerging hot from Provençal ovens. They also can be introduced at two different times to create a layering of flavors, one at the beginning of the long cooking, and then again shortly before the dish is finished (page 26).

Once harvested, the woody herbs keep longer than the green herbs do, maintaining their flavor, texture, and appearance for a week or more when stored, wrapped in plastic, in the crisper of the refrigerator.

Dried woody herbs are excellent kitchen pantry items. They are added in smaller amounts than when fresh because their volatile oils are intensified when the moisture has been removed. Dried herbs are best used in cooking where there is enough time for them to release and develop their flavor and to soften their texture. If added at the end of cooking they may contribute unappealing woody or papery bits and be too strong for some palates. This is particularly true of rosemary and sage. Directions for how to dry all the woody herbs are included on page 26.

BAY LAUREL (*Laurus nobilis*)

Also called sweet bay or Turkish bay, bay laurel can be found growing wild throughout much of the Mediterranean. It has also been incorporated into formal gardens such as the Alhambra Palace in Granada. It is so closely associated with Turkey that is sometimes called Turkish bay to distinguish it from California bay, *Umbellularia californica*, a different species with a leaf shape and pungent flavor that are similar.

Bay laurel is sweetly aromatic, and is used both fresh and dry to flavor soups and stews, plus vegetable and meat dishes that are baked or roasted. It is frequently used in marinades and is sometimes used with skewered meats, the leaves alternating with pieces of the meat. It is an essential flavoring for the varied fish soups that are indigenous to the Mediterranean.

Store it in the refrigerator in a plastic bag for up to a week to keep it fresh.

LAVENDER (*Lavandula* species)

Lavender is grown commercially in southern France primarily for its oil, which is used in the perfume trade, but the flowers and leaves, dried or fresh, are used as a flavoring in salads and in herb mixtures for meat rubs and marinades, as well as in sweets. They exude a strong, full sweet scent that is a little less pungent when dried. The seeds and ground stems are used to flavor goat cheese. Lavender is used primarily in Provence, where it is extensively cultivated and grows wild.

Store fresh lavender for a week or more in a plastic bag in the crisper of the refrigerator.

MARJORAM AND OREGANO
(*Origanum majorana* and *vulgare*)

Marjoram and oregano are closely related, so much so that oregano is also known as wild marjoram. Oregano is thicker stemmed, with more robust, larger leaves and a more pungent flavor. Both are Mediterranean natives. They are widely used in cuisines throughout the region and can be found both fresh and dried flavoring many dishes, from tomato sauces to all manner of cooked vegetables, stews, grills, and soups. Dried oregano is frequently used in salads and egg dishes. Cooks in Crete, Greece, Turkey, Lebanon, Spain, and Sicily favor these herbs.

Both herbs store well for a week or more in plastic bags in the crisper of the refrigerator.

ROSEMARY (*Rosmarinus officinalis*)

Rosemary, one of the most aromatic of herbs, is another Mediterranean native, an evergreen in warmer climates and an annual in colder areas. It has a wide array of uses, both fresh and dried. Cooks in Spain, southern France, and Italy all favor rosemary in their cuisines. Fresh, its resinous flavor is unsurpassed on meats, both grilled and roasted. It is a good counterpoint for full-flavored vegetables and can delicately flavor biscuits, poultry stuffings, and sausage mixtures.

Store fresh rosemary for a week or more in a plastic bag in the refrigerator, or in a glass of water set on a windowsill out of direct sunlight.

SAGE (*Salvia officinalis*)

Sage has long been used as a culinary herb. The fresh plant has an aromatic, slightly sharp taste that becomes more potent when it is dried. It is used to flavor rich meats and sausages and in stuffings. It also complements cooked vegetables and is used to flavor biscuits and breads. In kitchens in Crete, southern France, Spain, and Italy, cooks employ sage for grilling and seasoning long-simmered stews and soups, as well as to flavor breads.

Store fresh sage in a plastic bag in the crisper of the refrigerator for a week or so, or in a glass of water on a windowsill out of direct sunlight.

THYME (*Thymus vulgaris*)

This aromatic, low-growing, wiry bush is absolutely essential to Provençal cuisine, called for in almost every stew or other slow-cooked dish and grilled food. It is used fresh or dried with meat, poultry, cooked vegetables, sauces, and vinegars and is added fresh to a bouquet garni and dried to *herbes de Provence*. There are many species, including some that also have a flavor of lemon, nutmeg, or orange. A small handful of thyme thrust into a roasting chicken will imbue the bird with its subtle presence.

Put fresh thyme in a plastic bag and store in the crisper of the refrigerator, or slip into a glass of water and place on a windowsill out of direct sunlight.

WINTER SAVORY (*Satureja montana*)

Although culinarily very similar to summer savory, winter savory has a stronger and spicier flavor and stiffer leaves. It should be used with longer, slower-cooking, heavier dishes.

Winter savory is underutilized in the United States. It has a delicious peppery, woodsy fragrance and sharp taste that goes perfectly with, among other foods, beans and goat cheese, as the southern French have long known. In Provence, winter savory grows wild on the hillsides and is often called by its Provençal name, *pebre d'aie*, or "donkey's pepper." The sprigs are gently pressed into the surface of goat cheeses, where their flavor combines subtly with that of the cheese. It is an essential ingredient in *herbes de Provence* mixtures, or it can be used alone to season grilled meats, sauces, pizzas, breads, vegetables, soups, and stews.

Dried winter savory retains much of its deep, intense flavor and can be used throughout the cooking process, early, at the midpoint, or toward the end. Fresh winter savory holds onto its identity as well and can be added to simmered dishes such as fresh shelling beans, green beans, or tomato sauce, or to dishes that take anywhere from fifteen minutes to an hour to cook, like roasted chickens or grilled pork chops.

Store winter savory in a plastic bag in the crisper of the refrigerator, where it will keep for one week, or in a glass of water kept on a windowsill out of direct sunlight.

DRYING WOODY HERBS

Woody herbs may be dried in much the same manner as the green herbs. Gather a single variety into a loose bunch and tie with a length of kitchen string. Hang them in a cool, dark place with good air circulation. Once dried, the leaves can be stripped and stored in airtight containers. The stems, which are aromatic as well, can be slipped into paper bags and kept in a dry place. The stems can be added to grilling fires.

Kitchen Techniques

Here are a number of tips that will help you to bring out the flavors present in the foods you cook and to make the most of every herb's contribution. Included are how to cut fresh herbs, how to use herbs to create a layering of flavors, how to deep-fry and toast herbs, how to select a substitute when a particular fresh herb is not at hand, and how to enhance the flavors of prepared foods.

CUTTING FRESH HERBS

Herbs can be chopped in the kitchen using a chef's knife or double-handled, curved-bladed knife called a *mezzaluna*, or they can be snipped using kitchen scissors. I find scissors especially useful for rendering green herbs into small pieces, the *mezzaluna* excellent for cutting herbs into very fine bits, and a sharp chef's knife ideal for cutting the woody herbs.

In the garden, the tender green herbs can be cut with garden scissors or household scissors reserved for this task and the woody herbs with hand pruners.

LAST-MINUTE ADDITIONS

Adding fresh herbs, both green and woody, at the end of cooking, either stirring them in or sprinkling them on top of the hot soup, stew, sauté, vegetables, or fruits, will ensure that the herb's impact will be at its most intense, as the warmth of the food will release the flavor and aroma with no actual cooking necessary. Add fresh herbs to cold or room-temperature dishes during their preparation, allowing the flavors of the dish to blend a little, or, for a more intense flavor, add them just before serving, as you would a garnish.

LAYERING FLAVORS

In this technique, herbs are used twice or more at different times during the cooking, depending upon the length of the cooking time and the style of the preparation. Dried or fresh herbs, such as thyme and oregano, are added early in the preparation, to a stew for example, and then shortly before serving the same herbs are added again, this time fresh. This creates a depth of flavor that is especially desirable in long-simmering sauces, soups, stews, and in instances in which marinades have been used in the initial preparation. Herbs other than the original ones may be used as well in the second addition, particularly the green herbs. This adds a new flavor layer to the original.

DEEP-FRYING FRESH GREEN AND WOODY HERBS

Fresh herbs and their blossoms are wonderful deep-fried in oil. Only a few seconds are needed to produce a crispy, crunchy result that can then be incorporated into pasta dishes, salads, mixed fries, or as a distinctive garnish. No batter is needed.

Basil, parsley, arugula, and sage leaves are good candidates, as are sage, chive, and borage blossoms. In sprig form, chervil, parsley, basil, lovage, mint, thyme, sage, oregano, and marjoram are the most amenable to this treatment.

TOASTING DRIED AND FRESH WOODY HERBS AND DRIED GREEN HERBS

Add a sprinkle of dried herbs to a heated skillet to warm them and release their flavors before adding them to dishes where they will not be cooked, such as a salad dressing. Fresh woody herbs, those with resinous leaves, may be given the same treatment, but toasting is detrimental to the fresh green herbs.

SUBSTITUTIONS

Although most of the herbs are preferably used fresh, especially the green ones, there are times when fresh herbs are not available, and you will want to substitute dried ones in a recipe that calls for fresh. In general, use only one-third of the amount of

fresh. If using fresh herbs in place of dried, triple the amount.

Some of the more potent herbs, such as rosemary and sage, should be used even more sparingly when dried. Err on the side of too little until you know your herbs well. You can always add more, but it is impossible to add less.

Some of the green herbs lose their allure and flavor once dried, such as cilantro and chervil, so it is better, in my opinion, to substitute some other fresh herb. For example, if a recipe calls for cilantro and none is available, try using another fresh green herb, such as chives or parsley. The flavor will be slightly different, but the zing and character that fresh herbs deliver will be there. When this approach doesn't seem feasible, use the herb in its dried form, but remember the taste will be quite muted. In cases where fresh herbs are a major ingredient, such as sprigs or leaves in a salad, substitution of dried will simply not work and another dish should be considered.

USING HERBS WITH PREPARED FOODS

Commercially prepared foods of nearly every type can be enlivened by the use of fresh herbs, just as they would if you had prepared the dish from scratch in your own kitchen, then added the herbs just before serving. For example, green herbs can be tossed with fruit, vegetable, pasta, and green salads. Oregano, basil, rosemary, and thyme can be scattered over pizzas and other Italian foods. Vegetables, including potatoes, are amenable to a sprinkling of fresh basil, thyme, or rosemary. As you experiment, you will find your own favorites.

Small Dishes, Salads, and Soups

Part of the Mediterranean style of eating is the notion of little dishes. In southern France they are served as a first course, and in Italy you will find them as antipasti, the dishes that precede the main part of a meal. In Spain they make their appearance as tapas, originally bar food, but several plates can make a meal. In the eastern Mediterranean, these little dishes are called mezes, and can either precede a meal or in the case of a tableful, be the entire meal. Olives are nearly always served in every locale, and the little dishes can vary from garlic-rubbed toasts topped with chopped tomatoes and basil to baby octopus and fried squid and roasted vegetables. Their number and kind seem infinite.

Because vegetables, grains, and fruits are so important in the Mediterranean, it is not surprising that salads of these ingredients, well flavored with herbs, are a big part of any repast, whether in Italy, Greece, or Turkey. They might precede the meal, or a light green salad may follow the main course, particularly in France and Italy.

Soups, like salads, might begin a meal, while a particularly hearty soup, like Dried Fava Bean Soup with Fresh Bay and Spicy Meatballs (page 52) might serve as the focal point. Both light soups and substantial ones are included in this chapter.

As our eating habits change, I think the idea of eating a few little dishes, a salad, and perhaps some cheese and a simple dessert is an appealing alternative to a meal centered around a main dish.

Potato-Parsley Pancakes

Caponata

Omelet of Fines Herbes

Shrimp and Scallop Skewers
with Yogurt–Wild Fennel Marinade

Pork and Kumquat Skewers
with Dried Thyme and Lavender

Crostini with Cranberry Beans, Roasted Garlic,
and Winter Savory Spread

Summer Vegetables in Lemon
and Oregano Marinade

Minted Lamb Meatballs
with Fresh Green Herbs and Yogurt

Lentils and Potatoes with Bay Leaves

Rondelles of Fennel, Parmesan,
and Button Mushrooms on Parsley

Warm Artichoke Hearts
with New Potatoes and Borage Blossoms

Ragout of Potatoes and Wild Fennel Greens

Classic Tabbouleh

Black Olive and Squid Salad with Parsley and Mint

Saffron and Raisin Couscous with Fresh Mint

Tomato, Mozzarella, and Basil Salad

Oranges, Walnuts, and Watercress
with Lavender-Yogurt Dressing

Orange and Arugula Salad with Chicken

Salad of New Potatoes with Sweet Cicely,
Lovage, and Green Peppercorns

Orange Salad with Anchovies and Chives

Green Herbs and Butterhead Lettuce Salad

Green and Yellow Snap Bean Salad
with Summer Savory

Fava Bean Salad with Winter Savory

Dried Fava Bean Soup
with Fresh Bay and Spicy Meatballs

Soup of Fresh Fava Beans with Lovage and Mint Cream

Butternut Squash and Riso Soup with Fresh Oregano

Classic Gazpacho

Mediterranean Fish Soup

Eggplant and Tomato Soup
with Sage-Polenta Dumplings

Chilled Cucumber Soup with Dill and Chives

Chilled Melon Soup with Cilantro

Potato-Parsley Pancakes

Mashed potatoes, thickened with eggs and seasoned with herbs, are the basics of this rustic dish, which might be served as a tapa in Spain. Here, parsley is used, but lovage, dill, chives, or summer or winter savory would be equally good. Serve these golden brown cakes as a first course with sautéed apples, spinach, or chard or to accompany a main dish. They are also an appetizing choice for breakfast or brunch.

4 boiling potatoes such as White Rose, Yukon Gold,
  or Yellow Finn, peeled and cut into sixths

1½ teaspoons salt

¼ to ½ cup milk

1 tablespoon unsalted butter

2 eggs, lightly beaten

½ cup chopped fresh flat-leaf parsley

½ teaspoon freshly ground black pepper

⅓ cup all-purpose flour

1 tablespoon canola or other light vegetable oil, as needed

In a saucepan, combine the potatoes with water to cover by 2 inches. Add 1 teaspoon of the salt, bring to a boil over medium-high heat, then reduce the heat to low. Cook until the potatoes are tender when pierced with a fork, about 25 minutes. Drain off all but ¼ cup of the water.

Add ¼ cup of milk and the butter to the potatoes and mash with a potato masher or beat on low speed with a handheld mixer until fluffy, adding more milk if needed to achieve the desired consistency. Stir in the eggs, parsley, remaining ½ teaspoon salt, and the pepper until a thick paste forms.

Sprinkle half of the flour on a large sheet of waxed paper. Dust your hands with some of the remaining flour, then scoop up a handful of the potato mixture and form it into a patty about ½ inch thick. It will be sticky. Place the patty on the waxed paper and continue until the mixture is used up. You should have 8 to 10 patties in all. Dust the tops of the patties lightly with the remaining flour.

In a large, heavy-bottomed skillet, heat the oil over medium-high heat. When the oil is hot, reduce the heat to medium and slip as many patties into the skillet as will fit without touching. Cook on the first side until golden, 3 to 4 minutes. Turn and cook on the second side until golden, 2 to 3 minutes longer.

Remove to a platter in a warm oven and repeat with the remaining patties, adding more oil if necessary.

Serve immediately.

MAKES 8 TO 10 CAKES; SERVES 4

❀

Caponata

Full of the aroma of basil and olives, Sicilian caponata makes an excellent spread for crackers or toasted baguette slices.

¼ cup extra-virgin olive oil

1 large eggplant, peeled and cut into ½-inch cubes

4 tomatoes, peeled, seeded, and cut into ½-inch cubes

1 yellow onion, chopped

2 tablespoons chopped fresh basil, plus sprigs for garnish

2 tablespoons minced fresh lovage or celery leaves

¼ cup capers, drained

12 Sicilian or other Mediterranean-style green olives,
    pitted and coarsely chopped

1 to 2 tablespoons red wine vinegar

½ teaspoon salt

¼ teaspoon cayenne pepper

In a skillet, heat the olive oil over medium heat. When it is hot, add the eggplant cubes and stir until well coated with the oil. Cover, reduce the heat to low, and cook until the eggplant is very soft, about 15 minutes. Add the tomatoes and cook just until softened, about 3 minutes. Spoon the mixture into a large bowl and let cool to room temperature. Stir in the onion, chopped basil, lovage or celery leaves, capers, olives, vinegar, salt, and cayenne, mixing well.

Spoon into a serving bowl and garnish with basil sprigs.

MAKES ABOUT 2½ CUPS, ENOUGH FOR 30 TO
40 CRACKERS

❋

Omelet of Fines Herbes

Although fines herbes *are more closely associated with classical French cooking than with the Mediterranean table, one can always find an omelet like this one among the first courses in a Provençal bistro. It can also be served as the centerpiece of a light supper, especially when accompanied by* pommes frites.

6 eggs

¼ teaspoon salt

1 teaspoon freshly ground black pepper

1½ tablespoons unsalted butter

¼ cup *fines herbes* (page 125)

In a bowl, whisk together the eggs, salt, and pepper until frothy.

In a 12-inch skillet, melt the butter over medium heat. When it foams, add the eggs and stir until they begin to thicken, just a few seconds. Reduce the heat to low. As the eggs set along the sides, lift the edges with a spatula and tip the pan to let the uncooked egg run beneath. Continue to cook until the omelet is set, 30 to 40 seconds longer. The timing depends upon whether a slightly runny omelet or a firm omelet is preferred. The bottom should be slightly golden.

Sprinkle the *fines herbes* over one-half of the omelet to cover, leaving a 1-inch border uncovered along the edge. Slip a spatula under the uncoated half and, pulling the pan up and toward you, flip the uncoated half over the coated half. Cook for another 30 to 40 seconds, or until just set.

Remove to a warmed plate. Cut into three or four pieces and serve immediately.

SERVES 3 OR 4

Shrimp and Scallop Skewers with Yogurt–Wild Fennel Marinade

In the Mediterranean, this dish is made in summer or early fall, when the roadside fennel stalks sport broad umbrels of yellow blossoms. By then, the flavor of the stems and leaves is fully developed, and the yogurt readily absorbs it. An alternative is to use cultivated fennel bulbs or feathery leaves and crushed fennel seeds.

½ cup plain yogurt

4 wild or cultivated fennel stems, each 2 inches long, crushed

½ cup wild or cultivated fennel leaves, chopped

1 teaspoon fennel seeds, crushed, if not using wild fennel

1 tablespoon fresh lemon juice

½ teaspoon salt

½ teaspoon freshly ground black pepper

½ pound medium-sized shrimp, peeled and deveined

½ pound bay scallops

In a small bowl, combine the yogurt; fennel stems, leaves, and seeds (if using); lemon juice; salt; and pepper. Mix well, then add the shrimp and scallops and turn to coat them. Cover and refrigerate for at least 2 hours or for up to 4 hours.

Build a medium-hot fire in a grill. If using wooden skewers, soak 8 skewers in water to cover.

Thread the shrimp on the skewers alternately with the scallops. Place on the oiled grill rack and cook, turning once, just until the flesh is opaque throughout, about 1 minute on each side. Do not overcook.

Transfer to a platter or individual plates and serve hot.

MAKES 8 SKEWERS; SERVES 4

Pork and Kumquat Skewers with Dried Thyme and Lavender

Pork is especially amenable to the resinous flavors that flourish on the Provençal hillsides, and in this simple recipe that affinity is further exploited by mixing it with the tart, tangy sweetness of whole kumquats, a citrus fruit that thrives in the warm climates of the eastern Mediterranean. Using the dried lavender leaves and seeds, as well as the dried blossoms, creates a herbal, rather than perfumed, flavor. Crumble them between your fingertips or process them in a spice grinder before combining with the thyme and pepper.

1 teaspoon dried thyme leaves, crumbled

1 teaspoon dried lavender leaves, crumbled

¼ teaspoon lavender seeds and dried blossoms, crumbled

½ teaspoon freshly ground black pepper

¾ pound lean pork, cut into ½-inch cubes (about 24 cubes)

24 kumquats

In a small bowl, mix together the thyme; lavender leaves, seeds, and blossoms; and black pepper. Spread the mixture on a baking sheet lined with waxed paper or aluminum foil. Roll the pork cubes and the kumquats in the mixture and wrap them up in the paper or foil. Cover and refrigerate for 2 to 4 hours.

Build a medium-hot fire in a grill. If using wooden skewers, soak 6 wooden skewers in water to cover.

Thread the pork on the skewers alternately with the kumquats. Place the skewers on the oiled grill rack and cook until browned on the first side, 5 to 7 minutes. Turn and cook until the pork is nicely browned on the second side and just cooked through, 5 to 7 minutes longer.

Transfer to a warmed platter or individual plates and serve immediately.

MAKES 6 SKEWERS; SERVES 3 TO 6

❖

Crostini with Cranberry Beans, Roasted Garlic, and Winter Savory Spread

Nearly all beans are enhanced by the addition of winter savory. Cranberry beans have a rich, meaty flavor, and when they are pureed, as they are here, they make a thick and tasty spread. Large Spanish white beans could also be good prepared this way. Serve this spread warm or at room temperature on garlic-rubbed toasts of country-style bread.

   I cup dried cranberry beans, picked over and rinsed

   7 cups water

   1½ teaspoons salt, plus salt to taste

   I fresh bay leaf, or ½ dried bay leaf

   8 fresh winter savory sprigs, each 6 inches long,
      plus 2 tablespoons minced

   3 heads garlic, plus 4 cloves

   about ½ cup extra-virgin olive oil

   2 tablespoons fresh thyme leaves

   2 baguettes

   ½ teaspoon freshly ground black pepper

   minced roasted red sweet pepper

In a saucepan, combine the beans, water, 1 teaspoon of the salt, the bay leaf, and the winter savory sprigs. Bring to a boil over medium-high heat, reduce the heat to low, and simmer until the beans are soft, 2 to 2½ hours.

Meanwhile, preheat the oven to 300°F.

Cut off the upper one-fourth of the 3 whole garlic heads. Rub them all over with 2 tablespoons of the olive oil, then sprinkle with ½ teaspoon of the salt and the thyme. Place them in a baking dish in which they fit snugly. Bake until the cloves are thoroughly soft and can be pierced through to the heart with the tip of a sharp knife, 45 to 60 minutes. Remove and set aside. Raise the oven temperature to 400°F.

Cut the baguettes on the diagonal into pieces about ½ inch thick, and place the slices on a baking sheet. Bake until lightly golden, about 15 minutes. Turn and cook for another 10 minutes. Remove from the oven and turn the oven to broil. Brush the baguettes with 2 tablespoons of the olive oil and slip under the broiler until golden, 1 to 2 minutes. Remove from the broiler and let cool. Rub the toasts with the 4 garlic cloves. Set aside.

Drain the beans. (Reserve the liquid for another use, if desired.) Pinching at the base of each roasted garlic clove, squeeze out the garlic into a skillet. Add 1 tablespoon of the olive oil and the drained beans and place over medium heat. With the back of a spoon, mash the beans and garlic together and add the salt and pepper. Continue to mash, adding more olive oil as needed to form a smooth paste. Stir in the minced winter savory.

Spread each toast with about 1 tablespoon of the warm bean spread and garnish with a few bits of roasted pepper. Arrange on a platter and serve.

MAKES ABOUT 24 TOASTS; SERVES 6

NOTE: If the spread stands before serving, you will need to reheat it and add more olive oil to achieve a smooth, spreadable paste.

Summer Vegetables in Lemon and Oregano Marinade

Summer's abundant eggplants, peppers, tomatoes, and squashes are imports to the Mediterranean region from the New World. They make excellent candidates for the grill and from Turkey to Spain are traditional fare. One of the best picnics I have ever had was on a beach in Crete late one spring. We made a fire of grapevine prunings and grilled first the herbed vegetables and then the lamb, both of which we ate atop slabs of bread and washed down with local red wine.

I eggplant

2 red sweet peppers

2 zucchini

3 large red onions

I cup Lemon and Oregano Marinade (page 118)

Cut the eggplant lengthwise into slices ½ inch thick, then cut each slice in half. Cut the peppers in half lengthwise and discard the stems, seeds, and ribs. Slice the pepper halves lengthwise into strips 1 inch wide. Cut the zucchini lengthwise into slices ½ inch thick. Slice the onions crosswise into rounds ½ inch thick.

Carefully place the onions on the bottom of a shallow baking dish, followed by the rest of the vegetables. Add the sprigs of fresh thyme. Pour over the marinade. Turn the vegetables in the marinade, being careful not to break apart the onions. Cover and let stand at room temperature for 6 to 8 hours, turning the vegetables from time to time.

Build a medium-hot fire in a grill.

When the fire is ready, begin cooking the vegetables. Few grills are large enough to hold them all at once, so I suggest cooking those that take the longest first, starting with the eggplant slices. Remove them from the marinade and place them directly on the grill or in a hinged grilling basket. Cook until the underside is golden brown, about 6 minutes. If you have enough room on the grill, add the zucchini and turn the eggplant slices, cooking them until a golden crust has formed, another 4 or 5 minutes. Remove to a platter. Cook the zucchini until lightly browned, 3 to 4 minutes on each side. Remove to a platter and cook the red peppers and the onions. The onions will need 3 to 4 minutes on each side, and the peppers 2 to 3 minutes on each side.

Serve the vegetables hot or at room temperature.

SERVES 4 TO 6

❅

Minted Lamb Meatballs with Fresh Green Herbs and Yogurt

This is a version of a dish made by a friend who is an émigré from southern Iran, but it could be Turkish as well. The meatballs are always served with a bowl of yogurt and another of mixed green herbs—tarragon, mint, chives, and fenugreek. The yogurt is spooned alongside the meatballs and topped with the herbs. I offer the dish as an appetizer, but the recipe can easily be increased and the meatballs presented as a main course. The fragrant herbed cooking liquid in which the meatballs simmer makes a wonderful broth for cooking rice.

1 pound lean ground lamb

¼ cup fine dried bread crumbs

¼ cup minced yellow onion

2 cloves garlic, minced

1 egg, lightly beaten

2 tablespoons chopped fresh flat-leaf parsley, plus 1 large sprig

¼ cup chopped fresh mint, plus 1 large sprig

¾ teaspoon salt

½ teaspoon freshly ground black pepper

¼ teaspoon ground cardamom

⅛ teaspoon ground cinnamon

4 cups water

½ cup plain yogurt

FOR THE HERB TOPPING:

¼ cup chopped fresh tarragon

¼ cup chopped fresh mint

¼ cup chopped fresh chives

2 tablespoons fresh, young fenugreek (optional)

In a large bowl, combine the lamb, bread crumbs, onion, garlic, egg, minced parsley and mint, salt, pepper, cardamom, and cinnamon. Mix thoroughly. Shape the mixture into balls about the size of a walnut. You should have about 16 meatballs.

In a saucepan, bring the water to a boil over medium-high heat. Add the mint and parsley sprigs and reduce the heat to medium-low. Add the meatballs and simmer until no longer pink in the center, about 10 minutes. Scoop out the meatballs and place in a bowl. Reserve the cooking liquid for another use, if desired.

Spoon the yogurt into a small serving bowl. To make the topping, combine all the herbs in a separate bowl and stir well. Serve the meatballs hot or warm with the yogurt and the mixed green herbs.

MAKES ABOUT 16 MEATBALLS; SERVES 4

❈

Lentils and Potatoes with Bay Leaves

Bay trees (Laurus nobilis) *grow wild in the canyons of southern Europe, North Africa, and the Levant. In the Mediterranean climate that prevails at my home in northern California, I grow bay along my kitchen porch. The leaves have a sweet, delicate aroma that permeates cooked dishes and gives deep background flavor whenever they are used, as in this humble country dish. Small green-blue French lentils, sometimes called Puy lentils, hold their shape during cooking better than brown lentils do, so if you use the brown, keep an eye on them, as they can turn quickly from perfectly done to mushy.*

1 tablespoon olive oil

1 yellow onion, chopped

2 cloves garlic, minced

2 cups lentils (see recipe introduction),
  picked over and rinsed

3 fresh bay leaves, or 2 dried bay leaves

6 cups water

1 to 1½ teaspoons salt

2 boiling potatoes such as White Rose, Yukon Gold, or
  Yellow Finn, peeled or unpeeled, cut into ½-inch cubes

1½ teaspoons freshly ground black pepper

1 teaspoon fresh thyme leaves

In a saucepan, heat the olive oil over medium heat. When it is hot, add the onion and garlic and sauté until translucent, 2 to 3 minutes. Add the lentils and bay leaves, turning them in the olive oil until they glisten. Add the water and 1 teaspoon of the salt and bring to a boil. Reduce the heat to low and simmer, uncovered, for about 20 minutes. Add the potatoes and continue to simmer until most of the liquid is absorbed and the potatoes are tender, about 15 minutes longer. Just before serving, remove the bay leaves and discard. Stir in the pepper, thyme, the remaining ½ teaspoon of salt. Taste and adjust the seasoning. Spoon onto warmed plates and serve at once.

SERVES 6

✢

Rondelles of Fennel, Parmesan, and Button Mushrooms on Parsley

Flat-leaf parsley makes an excellent salad green when used in quantity, as it so frequently is in the Mediterranean, and it combines well with a number of different ingredients. It is often used in combination with fennel, a favorite Mediterranean vegetable.

5 tablespoons extra-virgin olive oil

5 tablespoons champagne vinegar

2 tablespoons minced shallot

½ teaspoon salt

½ teaspoon freshly ground black pepper

1 fennel bulb, trimmed

½ pound very firm white button mushrooms

1 ounce Parmesan cheese

2 cups fresh flat-leaf parsley leaves, coarsely chopped,
  plus whole leaves for garnish

In a large salad bowl, whisk together the olive oil, vinegar, shallot, salt, and ¼ teaspoon of the pepper. Taste and adjust the seasonings. Pour about one-fourth of the vinaigrette into a small bowl and set both bowls aside.

Using a mandoline if possible, or a chef's knife, cut the fennel bulb crosswise into paper-thin slices. You should have about 2 cups.

Cut each mushroom from the cap through the stem into paper-thin slices. Using a sharp knife or a vegetable peeler, shave the Parmesan into paper-thin slices or curls.

Put the chopped parsley in the bowl holding one-fourth of the vinaigrette and toss gently to coat. Add the fennel,

(recipe continues)

mushrooms, and three-fourths of the cheese to the salad bowl holding the remaining vinaigrette and toss gently to coat.

Divide the chopped parsley evenly among 4 individual plates. Spoon the fennel salad evenly over them. Top each with an equal amount of the remaining cheese, sprinkle with the remaining ¼ teaspoon pepper, and garnish with the whole parsley leaves. Serve at once.

SERVES 4

❈

Warm Artichoke Hearts with New Potatoes and Borage Blossoms

Borage blossoms, with their bright blue color and faint taste of cucumber, add a Sicilian note to a classic southern French combination of tender artichokes and new potatoes.

1½ pounds small new potatoes

1½ teaspoons salt

6 medium-sized artichokes

3 cups water mixed with

    2 tablespoons lemon juice or vinegar

⅓ cup extra-virgin olive oil

2 cloves garlic, minced

½ cup dry white wine

2 tablespoons fresh thyme leaves

½ teaspoon freshly ground black pepper

6 tablespoons red wine vinegar

¼ cup fresh borage blossoms

In a saucepan, combine the potatoes with water to cover by 2 inches. Add 1 teaspoon of the salt, bring to a boil over medium-high heat, and then reduce the heat to medium, cover, and cook until the potatoes are tender when pierced with a fork, about 25 minutes. Drain and set aside.

While the potatoes are cooking, prepare the artichokes. Working with 1 artichoke at a time, cut off the stem flush with the base and break off the tough outer leaves to reach the tender inner leaves. With a knife, trim away the tough, dark green layer where the outer leaves were attached to the base. Cut off the top one-third of the artichoke and discard, then cut the artichoke lengthwise into quarters. If the furry inner choke has developed to where it has prickles, scoop it out down to the heart with the edge of a spoon. Put the prepared artichokes into the lemon water.

In a skillet, heat 2 tablespoons of the olive oil over medium-high heat. Add the garlic and sauté for a minute or two, then add the artichokes. Reduce the heat to medium and sauté just until the artichokes begin to brown slightly, 3 or 4 minutes. Add the white wine and stir, scraping up any bits clinging to the bottom of the pan. Add the thyme leaves and ¼ teaspoons each of the salt and pepper, then reduce the heat to low and cover the skillet. Cook just until the base of the artichoke is tender enough to be pierced with the tip of a knife and nearly all the liquid has been absorbed. Remove from the heat and keep warm.

Thinly slice the still-warm potatoes and arrange the slices on 4 individual plates. Drizzle each plate with 1 teaspoon each of the olive oil and the vinegar, and sprinkle with the remaining ¼ teaspoon salt and pepper and half of the borage blossoms. Divide the warm artichokes and their pan juices evenly among the plates. Drizzle with the remaining olive oil and vinegar, and garnish with the remaining borage blossoms. Serve at once.

SERVES 4

Ragout of Potatoes and Wild Fennel Greens

This is my version of a wonderful dish I was served in a home on Crete. I later learned that it was a traditional springtime preparation that utilized the masses of lush wild fennel that line the roadsides and cover the hills during that season. It can be served as a first course or as the main dish of a simple lunch or supper, accompanied with bread and cheese.

2 tablespoons extra-virgin olive oil

½ yellow onion, chopped

6 boiling potatoes such as White Rose, Red Rose, Yellow Finn, or Yukon Gold, peeled or unpeeled, and quartered

2 cups chicken broth

1 dried bay leaf

½ teaspoon salt

½ teaspoon freshly ground black pepper

6 cups wild fennel fronds or 6 cups cultivated fennel fronds, plus ¼ teaspoon fennel seeds, crushed

In a large saucepan, heat the olive oil over medium heat. Add the onion and sauté until translucent, 2 to 3 minutes. Add the potatoes and sauté until they begin to glisten, 2 to 3 minutes. Pour in the chicken broth and stir in the bay leaf, salt, and pepper. Add the fennel, cover, reduce the heat to low, and simmer until the potatoes are tender and most of the liquid is absorbed, about 30 minutes.

Ladle into a warmed serving bowl and serve at once.

SERVES 4 TO 6

❋

Classic Tabbouleh

Tabbouleh, which originated in the Middle East, is a popular, grain-based Mediterranean salad with a large component of parsley and mint, which accounts for its refreshing taste and brilliant green hue.

2 cups water

1 teaspoon salt

5 teaspoons extra-virgin olive oil

1⅔ cups (10 ounces) bulgur

¼ cup fresh lemon juice

½ teaspoon freshly ground black pepper

1 cup chopped fresh mint

1 cup chopped fresh flat-leaf parsley

2 ripe tomatoes, seeded and diced

1 cucumber, peeled and minced

¼ cup chopped green onion

In a saucepan, combine the water, ½ teaspoon of the salt, and 1 teaspoon of the olive oil and bring to a boil. Put the bulgur in a heatproof bowl and pour the boiling water over it. Let stand, uncovered, for 1 hour.

In a large bowl, combine the remaining 4 teaspoons olive oil, the lemon juice, the remaining ½ teaspoon salt, and the pepper. Add the bulgur and mix well. Add the mint, parsley, tomatoes, cucumber, and green onion, and mix well once again. To allow the flavors to develop, cover and refrigerate for 2 hours or for up to 6 hours before serving.

SERVES 6 TO 8

❋

Black Olive and Squid Salad with Parsley and Mint

The crisp, clean flavor of the herbs enhances the mild taste of the squid and the salty tang of the olives in a dish you might find in Sicily, Tunisia, or Spain.

1½ pounds small squid (see note)

3 quarts water

1½ teaspoons salt

2 tablespoons fresh lemon juice

2 tablespoons extra-virgin olive oil

2 cloves garlic, minced

1 tablespoon red wine vinegar

½ red onion, thinly sliced

¼ cup chopped fresh flat-leaf parsley

¼ cup chopped fresh mint

⅓ cup salt-cured black olives, pitted and halved

½ teaspoon freshly ground black pepper

4 lettuce leaves

First, clean the squid: Working with 1 squid at a time, grasp the head just below the eyes and pull gently from the body. Using a sharp knife, slice off the tentacles from the rest of the head, then squeeze out the "beak" from the base of the tentacles. Set the whole tentacles aside. Slit the body pouch lengthwise and discard the quill-like cartilage and the entrails. Rinse the body well, peel off the mauve-patterned skin that covers it, then cut the body crosswise into ½-inch-wide pieces.

In a saucepan, combine the water and 1 teaspoon of the salt and bring to a boil over high heat. Add the squid and cook just until they turn opaque, about 1 minute. Drain and rinse immediately with cold water to prevent overcooking, which will toughen them. Drain again.

In a bowl, combine the remaining ½ teaspoon salt, the lemon juice, olive oil, garlic, vinegar, red onion, parsley, two-thirds of the mint, the olives, and the pepper. Mix well. Add the squid and toss well. Cover and refrigerate for at least 2 hours or for up to 6 hours.

Place a lettuce leaf on each of 4 individual plates. Spoon the salad onto the lettuce leaves, dividing evenly, and garnish with the remaining mint. Serve at once.

SERVES 4

NOTE: If you are purchasing already-cleaned squid, you will need about 1 pound.

✤

Saffron and Raisin Couscous with Fresh Mint

Couscous, a form of tiny pasta made from semolina, is common fare in Morocco, Tunisia, and Algeria and popular in France and Spain. It readily absorbs the flavors of herbs, and mint, parsley, and cilantro are frequently paired with it. Here, saffron, grown in Spain and parts of the eastern Mediterranean, is used along with mint to flavor this simple dish.

2 cups water

½ teaspoon saffron threads

1 teaspoon extra-virgin olive oil

½ teaspoon salt

2 cups (10 ounces) couscous

¼ cup raisins

3 tablespoons chopped fresh mint

In a saucepan, bring the water to a boil and add the saffron. Remove from the heat, cover, and let stand for 30 minutes.

Return the pan to the heat, bring to a boil, and mix in the olive oil, salt, couscous, and raisins. Remove from the heat, cover, and let stand for 30 minutes.

Using a fork and your fingertips, fluff the couscous to separate the grains. Taste and adjust the seasonings. Stir in the mint. Serve warm or at room temperature.

SERVES 8

❈

Tomato, Mozzarella, and Basil Salad

I frequently make this Italian classic during the summer with tomatoes and basil from my garden, sometimes even substituting tarragon for the basil. When the tomatoes are dead-ripe, there is no need for any vinegar, just a drizzle of very good extra-virgin olive oil. This can be made with any single variety of tomatoes—beefsteak, cherry, golden, orange, striped green—or a mixture, and with any of the different basil varieties. I especially like to pair purple basil with golden tomato for a stunning contrast.

½ pound fresh mozzarella balls packed in water

4 tomatoes, cut into ⅓-inch-thick slices

¼ to ⅓ cup fresh basil leaves

½ teaspoon freshly ground black pepper

¼ teaspoon salt

¼ cup extra-virgin olive oil

Remove the mozzarella balls from the water, and cut the balls into slices ⅓ inch thick. Arrange the tomato slices, basil leaves, and mozzarella slices on a platter. Sprinkle with the pepper and salt, then drizzle with the olive oil.

SERVES 4

❈

Oranges, Walnuts, and Watercress with Lavender-Yogurt Dressing

Oranges flourish along the shores of the Mediterranean, the lavender comes from the plateaus of Provence, and yogurt and honey are abundant throughout the area, so while this salad has no particular land of origin, I was inspired by the region's products.

2 oranges

1 teaspoon Dijon mustard

3 tablespoons honey

1 teaspoon minced fresh lavender blossoms,
   or ½ teaspoon dried lavender blossoms

½ cup low-fat plain yogurt

4 cups watercress leaves

1 cup coarsely chopped walnuts

Place 1 orange on a cutting board and cut a thick slice off the top and bottom to expose the flesh. Stand the orange upright and thickly slice off the peel, removing all the white pith and following the contour of the fruit. Cut the orange in half through the stem end, then slice crosswise. Repeat with the remaining orange. Place in a large salad bowl.

In a small bowl, beat the mustard into the honey, then add the lavender and yogurt, mixing well.

Add the watercress and half of the walnuts to the oranges and toss to mix. Then mix in the honey-yogurt dressing, turning gently. Spoon onto individual plates and garnish with the remaining walnuts.

SERVES 4

�֍

Orange and Arugula Salad with Chicken

The nutty, peppery flavor of young arugula, especially fresh from the garden, is well-matched with sweet, yet acidic, oranges, and adding cubes of chicken breast that have been rolled in savory bread crumbs and lightly fried in olive oil makes the salad a stellar one-dish meal.

¼ cup extra-virgin olive oil

1 clove garlic, minced

3 tablespoons red wine vinegar

½ teaspoon salt

½ teaspoon freshly ground black pepper

5 navel oranges

4 cups young, tender arugula leaves

1 cup seasoned bread crumbs

olive oil for frying

1 skinless, boneless whole chicken breast,
   cut into 1-inch cubes

In the bottom of a salad bowl, combine the extra-virgin olive oil and garlic and stir together. Whisk in the vinegar, salt, and pepper. Taste and adjust the seasonings.

Place 1 navel orange on a cutting board and cut a thick slice off the top and bottom to expose the flesh. Stand the orange upright and then thickly slice off the peel, removing all the white pith, and following the contour of the fruit. Cut along either side of each segment to free it from the membrane. Repeat with 3 more oranges; reserve the remaining orange for garnish. Cut the orange segments in half crosswise and add them to the bowl. If the arugula leaves are small, that is, 2 or 3 inches long, use them whole. If larger, tear each one into 2 or 3 pieces and add to the bowl.

Spread the bread crumbs on a sheet of waxed paper. In a large skillet, pour in olive oil to a depth of ½ inch and heat over medium heat. When it is hot, working in batches, roll the chicken cubes in the bread crumbs and slip them into the oil. Fry, turning once, until golden, about 2 minutes on each side. Remove with tongs and place on paper towels to drain. Add more oil to the pan as needed to fry all the chicken cubes.

Add the hot chicken cubes to the salad bowl. Mix well, turning deeply from the bottom of the bowl. Spoon portions from the bowl onto individual plates. Cut the remaining orange into eighths. Garnish each plate with 2 orange wedges and serve immediately.

SERVES 4

✤

Salad of New Potatoes with Sweet Cicely, Lovage, and Green Peppercorns

Here, sweet cicely's delicate fernlike leaves with their mild anise flavor, plus the celerylike taste of lovage, blend with a creamy dressing to create an intriguing potato salad.

2½ pounds new potatoes

1½ teaspoons salt

½ cup plain yogurt

½ cup low-fat sour cream

2 tablespoons mayonnaise

¾ cup chopped red onion

2 tablespoons chopped fresh sweet cicely

2 tablespoons chopped fresh lovage, plus 1 sprig for garnish

2 tablespoons green peppercorns

In a saucepan, combine the potatoes with water to cover by 2 inches. Add 1 teaspoon of the salt, bring to a boil over medium-high heat, and then reduce the heat to medium and cook, covered, until the potatoes are tender when pierced with a fork, about 25 minutes.

Drain the potatoes. As soon as you can handle them, peel and cut crosswise into ¼-inch-thick slices.

Place the potato slices in a large salad bowl and add the yogurt, sour cream, and mayonnaise. Turn well to mix. Add the remaining ½ teaspoon salt, the onion, sweet cicely, chopped lovage, and green peppercorns and turn again to mix. Cover and let cool to room temperature, then refrigerate for at least 6 hours and for up to 24 hours to allow the flavors to blend fully before serving.

Garnish with a sprig of lovage and serve.

SERVES 4

✤

Orange Salad with Anchovies and Chives

Algerian and Moroccan cooks frequently combine oranges, anchovies, and olives to make an appetizer. In this salad, chives are used instead of olives.

2 tablespoons fresh orange juice

2 tablespoons red wine vinegar

4 anchovy fillets, preferably salt-packed

1½ teaspoons extra-virgin olive oil

3 navel oranges

¼ cup chopped fresh chives

(recipe continues)

In a small bowl, combine the orange juice, vinegar, and anchovies. Using a fork, crush the anchovies and blend them into the liquid to make a thin paste. Alternatively, process the ingredients together in a small food processor.

Place 1 navel orange on a cutting board and cut a thick slice off the bottom to expose the flesh. Stand the orange upright and thickly slice off the peel, removing all the white pith and following the contour of the fruit. Cut along either side of each segment to free it from the membrane. Repeat with the remaining oranges. Cut the segments in half crosswise.

Put the orange segments in a large bowl with half the chives and turn to mix. Add the anchovy paste and turn again. Cover and refrigerate for at least 2 hours or for up to 24 hours. Garnish with the remaining chives just before serving.

SERVES 4 TO 6

NOTE: Salt-packed whole anchovies deliver better flavor and texture than fillets packed in oil, so use them here if possible. You will need to rinse the salt from 2 whole anchovies and fillet them to arrive at the 4 fillets needed here.

❖

Green Herbs and Butterhead Lettuce Salad

The mild flavor and delicate texture of butterhead lettuce makes an ideal background for the intense and distinctive flavors of the green herbs, which are used abundantly in salads in the Mediterranean. This is one of my favorite green salads, and I vary the herbs according to the season. In spring I use the plentiful chervil, parsley, and sorrel, while in early summer mint, cilantro, and tarragon take
over. In midsummer the emphasis is on basil, tarragon, dill, and cilantro, and in fall and winter, chicory and parsley appear. Sometimes I include only a single herb, other times a mixture. Of course, other lettuces and greens, like romaine, escarole, and curly endive, can be used as well. You can make the dressing in the bottom of the salad bowl and pile the lettuce and herbs on top. If they are not turned in the dressing, the salad can stand an hour before serving without wilting. When ready to serve, simply turn the greens to coat them.

¼ cup extra-virgin olive oil

1 tablespoon chopped shallot

2 tablespoons fresh lemon juice or red wine vinegar

½ teaspoon salt

½ teaspoon freshly ground black pepper

1 head butterhead lettuce, leaves separated

1 cup fresh chervil sprigs

½ cup fresh flat-leaf parsley leaves

¼ cup small, tender fresh sorrel leaves

In the bottom of a salad bowl, combine the olive oil and shallot and stir together. Whisk in the lemon juice or vinegar. Taste for balance. Add the salt and pepper and taste again, adjusting as desired.

Tear the lettuce leaves into bite-sized pieces, and put them into the bowl along with the chervil, parsley, and sorrel. When ready to serve, toss well.

SERVES 3 OR 4

❖

Green and Yellow Snap Bean Salad with Summer Savory

Snap beans, also known as green beans or, when pale yellow, wax beans, are a popular dish in southern France, where they dressed with a vinaigrette, seasoned with herbs, and served at room temperature. They might be a first course, either on their own or as one of two or more different preparations, or as an accompaniment to a main dish such as grilled fish or chops.

    ¼ cup fresh lemon juice

    ¼ cup extra-virgin olive oil

    1 teaspoon Dijon mustard

    2 tablespoons finely chopped summer savory

    1 teaspoon minced garlic

    ½ teaspoon sugar

    ½ teaspoon salt

    ¼ teaspoon freshly ground black pepper

    ¾ pound young, tender yellow snap beans, trimmed

    ¾ pound young, tender green snap beans, trimmed

In a large bowl, combine the lemon juice, olive oil, mustard, summer savory, garlic, sugar, salt, and pepper. Stir until just blended. Set aside.

Steam the beans until just tender, about 15 minutes. Remove from the steamer rack and place while still hot in the bowl with the vinaigrette. Turn to coat well.

Let stand at room temperature for 1 to 2 hours. Serve at room temperature.

SERVES 8

❋

Fava Bean Salad with Winter Savory

Fava beans, evidence of which has been found in the tombs of the pharaohs, are an Old World bean well known throughout Europe. They are used both fresh and dried and, like so many other beans, marry well with winter savory. Fresh fava bean salads appear in the Mediterranean in late spring and early summer when the legumes are still small and tender.

    8 cups water

    4 pounds young fava beans, shelled

    1 teaspoon salt

    2 fresh winter savory sprigs, plus 1 tablespoon minced

    2 tablespoons minced fresh chives

    ¼ cup extra-virgin olive oil

    1 teaspoon freshly ground black pepper

    1 cup young, tender arugula leaves

In a large saucepan, bring 4 cups of the water to a boil and plunge in the fava beans. Leave for 30 seconds, then drain. Let cool until they can be handled, then, with the tip of a knife, slit the skin of each bean along the seamlike edge and slip it off. You should have about 3 cups of beans.

In the same saucepan, combine the remaining 4 cups water, ½ teaspoon of the salt, and the winter savory sprigs and bring to a boil over medium-high heat. Add the peeled fava beans, reduce the heat to medium, and cook until the beans are just tender to the bite but still hold their shape, 5 to 10 minutes.

Drain the beans, then put them, still hot, in a bowl with the minced winter savory and the chives. Turn them well to coat. Add the olive oil, the remaining ½ teaspoon salt, and the pepper, and turn them well again.

(recipe continues)

Put a few arugula leaves on each of 4 individual plates, spoon the beans evenly over them, and serve immediately.

SERVES 4

❋

Dried Fava Bean Soup with Fresh Bay and Spicy Meatballs

Starchy, sturdy dried favas, a Spanish and Tunisian favorite, soak up the flavors of chiles, bay leaves, and garlic as they cook. Small meatballs made of sausage and amply seasoned with garlic and fresh parsley are cooked separately, then added to the soup just before serving.

FOR THE SOUP:

2 cups (¾ pound) dried fava beans, picked over and rinsed

8 cups water

1 yellow onion, chopped

6 cloves garlic, chopped

2 dried red chiles such as Colorado or New Mexico

2 tablespoons chopped fresh oregano

1 teaspoon salt

2 fresh bay leaves

FOR THE MEATBALLS:

¾ pound bulk pork or chicken sausage

½ teaspoon ground cumin

¼ teaspoon cayenne pepper

½ teaspoon salt

½ teaspoon freshly ground black pepper

1 clove garlic, minced

3 tablespoons minced fresh flat-leaf parsley

In a heavy soup pot, combine all the ingredients for the soup and bring to a boil over medium heat. Reduce the heat to low and simmer, uncovered, until the beans are tender but still hold their shape, about 2 hours.

While the beans are cooking, make the meatballs: In a bowl, combine all the ingredients and mix well. Shape the mixture into 1-inch balls. You should have about 12 balls.

Fill a saucepan half full with water, bring to a boil over high heat, then reduce the heat to medium. Using a slotted spoon, place the balls in the water and cook until they are no longer pink at the center, 6 to 8 minutes. Remove with the slotted spoon and set aside.

When the beans are done, remove the chile pods and bay leaves and discard. Add the sausage balls, heat through, and serve.

SERVES 6

❋

Soup of Fresh Fava Beans with Lovage and Mint Cream

Tender, young fava beans, treated to a gentle simmer in a lovage-flavored broth, then pureed with a little cream, make a sprightly beginning to a meal or, served with salad, a light supper dish. In most of the countries ringing the Mediterranean, the first fava beans appear in early spring, and these first of the season favas are considered a delicacy.

3 pounds young fava beans, shelled

3 cups chicken broth

2 tablespoons chopped fresh lovage or

¼ cup chopped celery leaves

½ teaspoon salt

½ teaspoon freshly ground black pepper

2 tablespoons heavy cream

1 tablespoon chopped fresh mint mixed with

   2 tablespoons crème fraîche or sour cream

4 fresh mint sprigs

Bring a saucepan half full of water to a boil. Plunge in the fava beans and leave for 30 seconds, then drain. Let cool until they can be handled, then, with the tip of a knife, slit the skin of each bean along the stemlike edge and slip it off. You should have a little over 2 cups of beans.

In the same saucepan, warm the broth over medium heat. When it is hot but not boiling, add the fava beans, all but 1 teaspoon of the lovage or celery, the salt, and the pepper. Cover, reduce the heat to medium-low, and cook until the beans are tender, 10 to 20 minutes. The timing will depend upon the age of the beans.

Pour the bean mixture into a blender or food processor and puree until smooth. Return the puree to the saucepan and stir in the cream. Place over medium heat and heat to serving temperature, but do not boil.

Ladle into warmed individual bowls. Top each serving with a spoonful of the mint-cream mixture, then garnish with a mint sprig. Serve at once.

SERVES 4

❉

Butternut Squash and Riso Soup with Fresh Oregano

This soup has a mellow background of flavors interwoven from sweet leeks, herbs, and caramelized bits of squash. They are simmered with Lillet Blanc, a French aperitif wine made from a white Bordeaux fortified with brandy and a secret ingredient or two. The rough, intense flavor of the oregano gathers all the elements together without overwhelming them.

1 large or 2 medium-sized butternut squashes,
   about 2 pounds total weight

2 tablespoons extra-virgin olive oil

½ teaspoon salt

½ teaspoon freshly ground black pepper

3 tablespoons fresh oregano leaves, chopped

⅓ cup Lillet Blanc, dry sherry, or dry white wine

2 tablespoons unsalted butter

1 large leek, including tender greens, chopped

4 cups chicken broth

½ cup *riso* pasta, cooked

Preheat oven to 350°F.

Cut the squash (or squashes) lengthwise. Scoop out the seeds and discard. Rub the cut sides all over with the olive oil and sprinkle with the salt, pepper, and half of the oregano. Place cut-side down in a baking pan and bake until the thickest part of the flesh is tender and easily pierced with a fork and the squash has browned and slightly caramelized on its cut surface, 1 to 1½ hours.

Raise the oven temperature to 450°F. Bake for 5 minutes longer, then remove from the oven.

(recipe continues)

While the squash halves are baking, melt the butter in a large saucepan over medium heat. When it foams, add the leek and sauté until translucent, 3 to 4 minutes. Add the chicken broth and bring to a boil. Reduce the heat to low and simmer for 10 minutes.

When the squash halves are ready, remove from the baking pan and set aside. Place the baking pan on the stove top over medium heat and pour in the wine. Cook, scraping up any bits clinging to the pan bottom, until the liquid is reduced to about 3 tablespoons. Pour the contents of the pan into the broth.

Scoop the flesh from the squash halves and add it to the saucepan. Whisk to the consistency of heavy cream. (Alternatively, process, in batches, in a blender or food processor.) Bring to just below a boil, stirring constantly. Add the cooked *riso*, stir, and simmer for 2 to 3 minutes.

Ladle the soup into warmed bowls and garnish with the remaining oregano. Serve immediately.

SERVES 4 TO 6

❉

Classic Gazpacho

Fresh herbs contribute much of the inimitable flavor for which this popular chilled Spanish soup is known. This recipe calls for cilantro, but flat-leaf parsley or basil is an equally fine complement to the tomatoes, cucumbers, and sweet peppers. While each herb brings its own distinctive flavor, the burst of freshness they deliver would be identical.

1½ cucumbers, peeled

3 large, firm ripe tomatoes, peeled

1 red bell or other red sweet pepper, seeded

2 teaspoons fresh lemon juice

1 tablespoon extra-virgin olive oil

1 clove garlic, crushed and minced

1½ tablespoons coarsely chopped fresh cilantro

½ teaspoon salt

1 teaspoon freshly ground black pepper

FOR THE CONDIMENTS:

1 cup Herb-Seasoned Croutons (page 95)

½ cucumber, peeled, seeded, and chopped

1 tomato, peeled and chopped

½ cup chopped pitted oil-cured black olives

⅓ cup chopped fresh cilantro

Coarsely chop the cucumbers, tomatoes, and red pepper. Place in a blender or food processor with the lemon juice and olive oil. Process until just blended and still slightly chunky. The mixture should not be a smooth puree. Pour into a nonreactive bowl and stir in the garlic, cilantro, salt, and pepper. Cover and refrigerate for at least 1 hour or for up to 6 hours.

To serve, divide the croutons among 4 bowls. Put the remaining condiments in separate bowls on the table. Pour the gazpacho over the croutons, dividing evenly, and serve at once. Let diners add the remaining condiments as desired.

SERVES 4

❉

Mediterranean Fish Soup

Along the western Mediterranean coast, this soup is served in various guises, depending upon the country and the region, but typically it is made with the poorer, smaller fish of the local waters. The broth is thickened with potato, seasoned with wild fennel and other herbs, and then passed through a food mill. The resulting soup is an unctuous, coral-colored puree traditionally accompanied with garlic toasts and a bowl of spicy pepper sauce.

¼ cup extra-virgin olive oil

2 yellow onions, chopped

3 cloves garlic, chopped

1 fennel stalk with leaves, 10 inches long, chopped,
   or ½ cup chopped fennel bulb

3 potatoes, peeled and cut into pieces

2 to 3 pounds whole fish such as smelt, rock cod,
   or snapper, cleaned but heads and tails left intact

2 or 3 small rock crabs (optional)

3 tomatoes, peeled

3 fresh thyme sprigs, each 6 inches long

2 fresh bay leaves, or 1 dried bay leaf

1 piece dried orange peel, 2 inches long

1 teaspoon salt

1 teaspoon freshly ground black pepper

8¼ cups water

2 cups dry white wine

12 slices baguette or coarse country bread, toasted and
   rubbed with garlic

½ cup Red Pepper Sauce (page 113)
   seasoned with ¼ teaspoon cayenne pepper

In a heavy soup pot, heat the olive oil over medium heat. Add the onions, garlic, and fennel and sauté until beginning to soften, 2 to 3 minutes. Add the potatoes, the whole fish, and the crabs, if using, and continue to cook until the fish has colored and started to fall apart, 4 to 5 minutes longer. Stir in the tomatoes, thyme, bay, orange peel, salt, pepper, 8 cups of the water, and the wine. Bring to a boil, then reduce the heat to low, and simmer, uncovered, for 20 minutes. Remove from the heat. Pass the contents of the soup pot through a food mill placed over a clean saucepan to extract the juices and the essence of the ingredients. Set the resulting puree aside. Return the pomace trapped in the food mill to the original soup pot and add the remaining ¼ cup water. Place over medium heat and cook, stirring, for 3 or 4 minutes. Pass the pomace through the food mill placed over the saucepan holding the puree, extracting more juice and essence. Discard the pomace in the food mill.

Heat the contents of the saucepan over medium heat and cook, stirring, until it thickens, about 5 minutes. Do not allow it to become pastelike. Taste and adjust the seasonings.

Place a slice of toast in each soup bowl and ladle the hot soup over it. Serve accompanied with the remaining toasts and the red pepper sauce, to be spooned over the soup as desired.

SERVES 4

Eggplant and Tomato Soup with Sage-Polenta Dumplings

Sage and thyme are the flavoring herbs in this substantial soup. They season the eggplant, which is oven roasted in cubes that are eventually added to the soup, much like croutons. Sage flavors the polenta, and both thyme and sage accent the soup to create an agreeable breadth of Italian tastes.

FOR THE SOUP:

1 eggplant, ½ to ¾ pound, cut in ½-inch cubes

5 tablespoons extra-virgin olive oil

1 teaspoon salt

1 teaspoon freshly ground black pepper

2 teaspoons minced fresh thyme

1 teaspoon minced fresh sage

2 cloves garlic, minced

6 pounds ripe tomatoes, peeled, seeded, and
   coarsely chopped

1 cup chicken broth

FOR THE POLENTA:

4 cups water

1 teaspoon salt

½ cup polenta (yellow cornmeal)

2 tablespoons unsalted butter

2 tablespoons grated Parmesan cheese

¼ cup chopped fresh sage

½ teaspoon freshly ground black pepper

Preheat an oven to 400°F.

To make the soup, in a medium bowl, combine the eggplant, 3 tablespoons of the olive oil and half each of the salt, pepper, thyme, and sage. Turn to coat well. Spread the cubes in a single layer on a baking sheet and bake until softened, about 10 minutes. Turn and bake until lightly golden, another 10 minutes. Remove from the oven and set aside.

In a heavy saucepan, heat the remaining 2 tablespoons olive oil over medium-high heat. Add the garlic and sauté until translucent, 1 to 2 minutes. Add the tomatoes and the remaining salt, pepper, thyme, and sage. Bring to a boil, reduce the heat to low, and simmer, uncovered, until the tomatoes are reduced by half, about 40 minutes. Add the chicken broth and cook for another 15 minutes to thicken.

While the soup is cooking, make the polenta: In a saucepan, bring the water and salt to a boil over high heat. Add the polenta in a slow, steady stream, whisking constantly. Reduce the heat to low and cook, stirring frequently, until the polenta has stiffened and begun to pull away slightly from the sides of the pan, about 40 minutes. Stir in the butter, cheese, sage, and pepper. Pour into a bowl and let stand until firmly set, about 20 minutes.

Measure out 1 cup of the tomato soup, ¼ cup of the eggplant, and 1 tablespoon of the polenta and place in a blender. Puree until smooth, then add to the soup. Using a melon baller, scoop out balls of the polenta and drop them into the hot tomato soup. Add the eggplant cubes and the remaining herbs and simmer just long enough to heat the polenta and eggplant through, 3 to 4 minutes.

Ladle into warmed bowls and serve at once.

SERVES 6

�֍

Chilled Cucumber Soup with Dill and Chives

Cool, delicate, and laced with a harmony of green herbs, this soup is one you might sample in Turkey or Greece on a hot summer day, sipping it in the deep shade of a spreading tree.

1½ cups peeled, diced cucumber

2 tablespoons extra-virgin olive oil

1 tablespoon minced red onion

1 clove garlic, minced

1 tablespoon white wine vinegar or champagne vinegar

3 tablespoons chopped fresh dill

1 teaspoon chopped fresh chives

½ teaspoon salt

½ teaspoon freshly ground black pepper

1½ cups plus 2 tablespoons plain yogurt

½ cup chilled chicken broth

3 or 4 ice cubes

In a bowl, combine the cucumber, olive oil, onion, garlic, vinegar, 2 tablespoons of the dill, the chives, salt, and pepper. Stir well, cover, and refrigerate for at least 3 hours or for up to 5 hours before serving.

When ready to serve, stir in the yogurt and the chilled broth. Ladle into bowls, add an ice cube to each, garnish with an extra dollop of yogurt, and sprinkle with the remaining 1 tablespoon dill.

SERVES 3 OR 4

Chilled Melon Soup with Cilantro

The color of your soup, of course, will depend upon the color of the flesh of the melon that you choose. The soft salmon of a cantaloupe, the palest lime of a honeydew, and the near ivory of a Galia will all show off the bright green specks of cilantro, a Tunisian standby, added at the finish. For a slightly different finish you might choose fresh mint or basil.

1½ cups water

1 cup fruity white wine such as Chenin Blanc,
   Sémillon, or Gerwürztraminer

¼ cup sugar

1 teaspoon grated lemon zest

1 ripe melon such as cantaloupe, honeydew, or Galia,
   about 2 pounds, halved, seeded, peeled, cubed, and chilled

1 ice cube

2 tablespoons minced fresh cilantro

In a saucepan, combine the water, wine, sugar, and half of the lemon zest. Bring to a boil over medium-high heat. Continue to boil until the liquid is reduced by about one-third. Remove from heat, let cool, and then place in the freezer for 15 minutes to chill.

In a blender or food processor, combine half of the wine mixture, half of the melon cubes, and the ice cube. Puree until smooth. Pour into a soup tureen. Repeat with the remaining wine mixture and melon cubes and add to the first batch. Stir in the remaining lemon zest and all but 1 teaspoon of the cilantro.

Ladle into chilled bowls and garnish each serving with a little of the remaining cilantro. Serve at once.

SERVES 6

Main Courses

    Lamb, fish, shellfish, poultry, and the occasional veal are the favored ingredients for main dishes in the Mediterranean. It is easy to imagine the myriad different treatments these might be given. I've chosen to focus here primarily on simple Mediterranean and Mediterranean-inspired presentations rather than on renditions of traditional dishes, which can be quite complex. A tajine from Morocco, Spanish paella, and a North African stuffed lamb breast are the exceptions, though even these are not difficult, just a little time-consuming.

    A bit of fish roasted with rosemary, shellfish steamed and scattered with parsley or cilantro, or a chicken steeped in spiced broth are all examples of the ease of Mediterranean cooking. In smaller portions, the shellfish might be served as a first course, as is true of many of the other offerings in this chapter.

Moules Marinière

Clams in Herbed Broth

Roasted Monkfish Tails with Fava Beans,
Winter Savory, and Tomatoes

Oven-Roasted Mussels with Spicy Cilantro Sauce

Grilled Sea Bass in
White Wine and Coriander Sauce

Sea Bass in Herbed Saffron Broth with Riso

Halibut Kabobs
with Winter Savory and Lemon

Foil-Wrapped Halibut Roast Infused with Rosemary

Grilled Cornish Hens
with Thyme and Winter Savory

Roasted Chicken with Sage and Rosemary

Moroccan Spiced Chicken

Lamb and Artichoke Tajine

North African Stuffed Lamb Breast

Lamb Shank and Dried Fruit Braise

Veal Shanks with Lemon,
Capers, and Thyme

Classic Paella

Provençal Tart with
Bacon, Ham, and Young Greens

Pasta with Pressed Purple Basil
Leaves and Blossoms

Mussel Risotto
Flavored with Garlic and Thyme

Fettuccine with Tomatoes, Capers, and Oregano

Pappardelle with Fried Basil Leaves
and Serrano Ham

Moules Marinière

This classic Mediterranean dish has many versions. I am especially fond of one made by a friend from Marseilles who scatters freshly grated garlic and fresh thyme over the mussels just as they start to steam. As the mussels open, their sea-salty juices mingle with the wine, thyme, and garlic, producing a seductive broth. If you have enough mussels left over, use them and the broth to make Mussel Risotto Flavored with Garlic and Thyme (page 84).

1 tablespoon extra-virgin olive oil

1 tablespoon unsalted butter

½ yellow onion, chopped

4 to 5 pounds mussels, scrubbed and debearded

¾ cup dry white wine

1 teaspoon fresh thyme leaves

3 cloves garlic

In the bottom of a large pot, combine the olive oil and butter and place over medium-high heat until they foam. Add the onion and sauté until translucent, 2 to 3 minutes. Add the mussels and pour in the wine. Rub the thyme between your hands over the pot, allowing it to fall over the mussels, then grate the garlic over the mussels. Cover, reduce the heat to low, and cook just until the mussels open, 10 to 12 minutes. Uncover and turn them in the broth.

Using a large slotted spoon, scoop the mussels into individual bowls, discarding any that failed to open. Ladle some broth into each bowl and serve at once.

SERVES 4

Clams in Herbed Broth

Once they are hot, the clams take only minutes to open, and large bowls of them can be served, with their broth, Mediterranean seaside–style. The herbs here can be varied to produce different flavors, using parsley only instead of parsley and thyme to produce a milder liquid, or thyme and oregano for a more potent one. Be sure to have plenty of bread for sopping up the broth.

1 tablespoon extra-virgin olive oil

1 tablespoon unsalted butter

2 cloves garlic, minced

½ yellow onion, minced

4 or 5 fresh thyme sprigs, each 6 inches long,
   or 1 or 2 dried thyme sprigs

6 pounds clams, scrubbed

¾ cup dry white wine

2 tablespoons chopped fresh flat-leaf parsley

In the bottom of a large pot, combine the olive oil and butter and place over medium heat until they foam. Add the garlic and onion and sauté until translucent, 2 to 3 minutes.

Rub the thyme between your hands, over the pot, allowing it to fall over the onion and garlic. Add the clams and the white wine, stir, cover, reduce the heat to low, and cook until the clams open, about 10 minutes. Uncover, sprinkle on the parsley, and stir to mix.

Using a large slotted spoon, scoop the clams into 4 individual bowls, discarding any that failed to open. Ladle some broth into each bowl and serve at once.

SERVES 4

Roasted Monkfish Tails with Fava Beans, Winter Savory, and Tomatoes

Meaty, lobsterlike monkfish, popular on the Mediterranean table, is seasoned with a variety of different herbs, depending upon the presentation and other ingredients. It is a good choice for roasting, as it holds its shape and remains firm during cooking.

2 pounds fava beans, shelled

½ cup all-purpose flour

2 cloves garlic, minced

1 teaspoon fresh thyme leaves

1 teaspoon minced fresh winter savory,
  plus 1 sprig

1 teaspoon salt

1 teaspoon freshly ground black pepper

4 monkfish tails, each about ⅓ to ½ pound

1 tablespoon extra-virgin olive oil

2 cups dry white wine

4 ripe tomatoes, peeled, seeded,
  and coarsely chopped

Preheat an oven to 450°F.

Bring a saucepan half full of water to a boil. Plunge in the fava beans, leave for 30 seconds, then drain. Let cool until they can be handled, then, with the tip of a knife, slit the skin of each bean along the seamlike edge and slip it off. You should have a little over 1 cup of beans. Set aside.

In a bowl, combine the flour, garlic, thyme, minced winter savory, salt, and pepper. Mix well and coat the fish with the mixture.

Oil the bottom of a shallow roasting pan with the olive oil and add the fish. Roast for 5 minutes, then add 1 cup of the white wine, the fava beans, and half of the tomatoes. Roast the fish, turning it once or twice in the sauce, until it is opaque and tender throughout, about 20 minutes.

Remove the fish to a platter and cover loosely with aluminum foil. Put the roasting pan on the stove top over high heat and add the remaining 1 cup white wine and the remaining tomatoes. Cook, stirring to scrape up any bits clinging to the bottom of the pan. Bring to a boil and cook until the liquid is reduced by half, 2 to 3 minutes.

Pour the sauce over the fish and garnish with the winter savory sprig. Serve immediately.

SERVES 4

Oven-Roasted Mussels with Spicy Cilantro Sauce

Mussels are standard fare in the Mediterranean countries, and there are many, many ways to prepare them. Here, they are a main course, and all that is needed is bread for dipping. The chiles are typical of the seasonings in Spanish and Moroccan cooking.

FOR THE SAUCE:

3 cloves garlic

2 green serrano chiles, seeded and chopped

¼ teaspoon salt

1 tablespoon extra-virgin olive oil

1 teaspoon fresh lemon juice

¼ teaspoon freshly ground black pepper

½ cup minced fresh cilantro

½ cup mayonnaise

rock salt for roasting

3 pounds mussels, scrubbed and debearded

Preheat an oven to 500°F.

To make the sauce, in a blender or food processor, combine the garlic, chiles, salt, olive oil, lemon juice, and pepper. Process to a smooth puree. Pour into a bowl and add the cilantro and mayonnaise. Stir to mix well. Cover and refrigerate until needed.

Make a bed of rock salt about 1½ inches deep in a heavy ovenproof skillet or baking dish. Place in the oven for 15 minutes to heat the salt thoroughly. Remove from the oven and arrange the mussels in a single layer on top of the salt. Return to the oven and roast just until the mussels open, 5 to 7 minutes.

Remove from the oven and transfer the mussels to a platter, discarding any that failed to open. Pass the sauce at the table.

SERVES 4

❀

Grilled Sea Bass in White Wine and Coriander Sauce

Sea bass is especially flavorful and its firm texture lends itself to grilling, but other firm, white-fleshed fish such as halibut or monkfish might be used here as well. The flavor of the coriander, which infuses the light sauce, finds an echo with the sprinkling of fresh cilantro.

FOR THE SAUCE:

1 tablespoon unsalted butter

2 tablespoons minced shallot

1 teaspoon coriander seeds, crushed

¼ cup chopped fresh cilantro

1 cup dry white wine

2 tablespoons fresh lime juice

FOR THE FISH:

1 tablespoon freshly ground coriander

1 teaspoon salt

1 teaspoon freshly ground black pepper

2 tablespoons extra-virgin olive oil

4 sea bass fillets, each about ¼ pound and 1 inch thick

1 fresh cilantro sprig

Build a medium-hot fire in a grill.

To make the sauce, in a small saucepan, melt the butter over medium heat. Add the shallot and sauté until translucent, 2 to 3 minutes. Add the coriander seeds, half of the chopped cilantro, the white wine, and the lime juice. Raise the heat to high and bring to a boil. Cook until the liquid is reduced by half, 3 to 4 minutes. Remove from the heat and set aside.

To prepare the fish, in a small bowl, mix together the ground coriander, salt, pepper, and olive oil to make a paste. Rub the fish fillets evenly with the paste. Place the fish on the oiled grill rack and cook on the first side until golden, about 7 minutes. Turn and cook on the second side until firm and opaque throughout, 5 to 6 minutes.

While the fish is cooking, reheat the sauce over medium heat and add the remaining chopped cilantro. Remove the fish to a warmed platter and pour the hot sauce over the fish. Garnish with the cilantro sprig, and serve at once.

SERVES 4

❈

Sea Bass in Herbed Saffron Broth with Riso

A light soup, flavored with green herbs, brings the taste of the Mediterranean to your table in a delicate ocher broth enriched with tiny riso *pasta and bites of meaty sea bass and garnished with lovage, a Tunisian favorite.*

4 cups chicken broth

½ teaspoon saffron threads

¼ cup minced fresh flat-leaf parsley

¼ cup minced fresh chives

2 tablespoons minced fresh lovage or celery leaves, plus 8 to 12 whole leaves for garnish

½ teaspoon salt

⅓ teaspoon freshly ground black pepper

¼ cup *riso* or other tiny pasta

1½ pounds sea bass fillet, cut into 1-inch cubes

1 large ripe tomato, peeled, seeded, and diced

Put the chicken broth and saffron in a saucepan and bring to a boil. Remove from the heat and let stand for 30 minutes.

Return the saucepan to medium heat and add the parsley, chives, minced lovage or celery, salt, and pepper. Bring to a boil and add the pasta. Reduce the heat to low and cook for 7 minutes. Add the sea bass and cook until the fish is opaque throughout, 2 to 3 minutes. Stir in the tomato.

Ladle into bowls and garnished with the whole lovage or celery leaves.

SERVES 4

❈

Halibut Kabobs with Winter Savory and Lemon

Winter savory, which is so important in flavoring beans, is also an excellent seasoning for firm, meaty fish that can be cubed. Kabobs are a common way to cook fish in the Mediterranean region, where they are often treated to an herbed marinade or rub before grilling.

2 pounds halibut fillet, about 1 inch thick,
   cut into 1-inch cubes (about 40 cubes)

grated zest of 1 lemon

2 tablespoons fresh lemon juice

4 or 5 fresh winter savory sprigs, each about
   4 inches long, plus 1 teaspoon minced

½ teaspoon salt

½ teaspoon freshly ground black pepper

Put the cubed halibut in a bowl and add the lemon zest, lemon juice, winter savory sprigs, minced winter savory , salt, and pepper. Turn the cubes to coat them. Cover and refrigerate for 20 to 30 minutes.

Build a fire in a grill. If using bamboo skewers, soak 8 skewers in water to cover.

Thread the halibut cubes onto the skewers. Discard the winter savory sprigs. Place the skewers on an oiled grill rack 5 or 6 inches from the heat source, and grill, turning once, until golden on the outside and just opaque throughout, about 5 minutes on each side.

Remove to a warmed platter and serve at once.

SERVES 8

Foil-Wrapped Halibut Roast Infused with Rosemary

The fish, foil-wrapped and steamed on a grill, emerges succulent and flaky, permeated with the taste of rosemary. It can be accompanied with a simple green vegetable such as chard or spinach and roasted tomatoes. You might consider using other woody herbs, such as thyme, oregano, or marjoram, in place of the rosemary. The roast itself is the equivalent of several fish steaks, and can be ordered in advance from your local fishmonger.

1 halibut roast, about 3½ pounds

1 teaspoon salt

1 teaspoon freshly ground black pepper

2 tablespoons unsalted butter

4 fresh rosemary sprigs, each 4 inches long

melted unsalted butter and lemon wedges

Build a medium-hot fire in a grill with a cover.

Rub the roast all over with the salt and pepper. Place on a sheet of heavy-duty aluminum foil and rub the ends and the top of the foil with 1 tablespoon of the butter. Then pack the bone on each end with ½ tablespoon butter. Put 2 rosemary sprigs on each end and wrap the roast tightly in the foil.

Put the foil package, seam side down, in the center of the grill rack. Cover and cook for 10 minutes per pound for a roast that is 6 inches thick, another 1 to 2 minutes per pound for roasts up to 8 inches thick.

Remove the foil, seam side up, to a platter. Peel back the foil and the skin will peel back with it, leaving the succulent flesh exposed. To check for doneness, insert a knife all the way to the bone in the center of the roast. There should be no pink

(recipe continues)

remaining and the meat should easily pull away from the bone. If not, rewrap the fish and return it to the grill for another few minutes.

Fillet the fish in 4 pieces, 2 pieces from the upper half and 2 pieces from the lower. Cut each piece in half to make 8 pieces in all. Discard the bones and skin. The juices from the fish, although they look tempting, are diluted and lacking in flavor. Instead, serve the fish with lemon wedges and a bowl of melted butter.

SERVES 6 TO 8

Grilled Cornish Hens with Thyme and Winter Savory

Butterflied Cornish hens, well seasoned with sprigs of fresh thyme and winter savory, cook quickly on an outdoor grill. These browned birds might be served with roasted potatoes, or a couscous or rice dish, accompanied by a tomato or cucumber salad. For dessert, a simple fruit custard or baked fruit would be appropriate.

FOR THE GIBLET GRAVY:

giblets from 2 Cornish hens

1 carrot, halved

1 celery stalk, halved

1 large yellow onion

2 fresh bay leaves, or 1 dried

½ teaspoon salt, plus salt to taste

½ freshly ground black pepper,
  plus pepper to taste

3 to 4 cups water

¼ cup dry white wine

1 tablespoon cornstarch
  mixed with 1 tablespoon water

2 Cornish hens

1 teaspoon freshly ground black pepper

½ teaspoon salt

8 fresh thyme sprigs

4 fresh winter savory sprigs

To make the giblet gravy, in a saucepan, combine the giblets, carrot, celery, onion, bay, ½ teaspoon each salt and pepper, and 3 cups of the water. Bring to a boil, reduce the heat to low, and simmer, uncovered, for 1 hour, adding more water if needed to cover. Remove from the heat. Lift out and discard the vegetables. Remove the giblets and mince them. Set aside. Return the pan to medium heat and boil until reduced to ¾ cup. Then add the wine and again boil until reduced to ¾ cup. Remove from the heat, add the giblets, and set aside until ready to serve.

Build a medium-hot fire in a grill with a cover.

With poultry shears, scissors, or a heavy knife, cut through the breastbone from the neck to the tail of each hen and spread each butterflied hen flat. Rub both sides of the hens with the pepper and salt and then with the fresh thyme and winter savory sprigs. Place them, skin side down, on an oiled grill rack and sear for 2 to 3 minutes, then turn and sear on the other side for 2 to 3 minutes. Continue to grill, turning often, for another 8 to 10 minutes. Using tongs, remove the birds to a platter. Remove the grilling rack from the grill and set aside. Push the coals to the sides of the grill pan and place a drip pan in the bottom of the grill, surrounded by the hot coals. Replace the rack. Return the hens to the rack, placing them skin side up over the drip pan. Put the cover on the grill and open the vent holes on the lid and at the bottom. Cook until the flesh is white and firm and the skin is crispy and golden, 5 to 10 minutes longer.

Meanwhile, reheat the gravy liquid over low heat. Stir the cornstarch mixture into the hot liquid until the mixture thickens, just a minute or so. Season with salt and pepper. Keep warm. Remove the hens from the grill, split each hen in half, and place on a platter or individual plates. Pour the gravy into a bowl and pass at the table.

SERVES 4

❧

Roasted Chicken with Sage and Rosemary

The herbs infuse the chicken as it slowly roasts, filling the kitchen with a heady aroma. Nothing could be simpler to prepare than this classic bird, which is often found on Sunday tables in Provence and Italy.

1 chicken, about 3 pounds

½ teaspoon salt

½ teaspoon freshly ground black pepper

4 or 5 fresh sage sprigs

4 fresh rosemary sprigs, each 2 inches long

Preheat an oven to 350°F.

Rinse the chicken, pat dry, and then rub inside and out with the salt and pepper. Rub the outside all over with the sage sprigs, then put them in the cavity. Rub the outside with the rosemary as well, but add only two of the lengths to the cavity, discarding the other two. Put the chicken in a roasting pan.

Roast until the skin is crispy golden, the meat is cooked through and the juices no longer run pink when a knife is inserted at the base of the thigh, 1¼ to 1½ hours.

Remove to a platter, cover loosely with aluminum foil, and let stand for 10 minutes before carving. Carve at the table.

SERVES 4

❧

Moroccan Spiced Chicken

In Moroccan cooking, cilantro and parsley are commonly used herbs, often in quantity, along with the spices cumin, saffron, and cinnamon. Here, a chicken is simmered whole in a sauce laden with herbs and spices and then the sauce is reduced and poured over the tender meat. Serve with couscous or rice and a simple green salad.

4 tablespoons unsalted butter

1½ yellow onions, sliced

4 cloves garlic, minced

1 chicken, about 3 pounds

1 teaspoon ground ginger

½ teaspoon ground cumin

4 cups water

½ teaspoon freshly ground black pepper

½ teaspoon saffron threads

½ teaspoon salt

½ cinnamon stick

1 large bunch fresh cilantro, tied, plus sprigs for garnish

1 large bunch fresh flat-leaf parsley, tied

In a large pot, melt the butter over medium-high heat. When it foams, add the onions and the garlic and sauté until the onion is translucent, 2 to 3 minutes. Remove with a slotted spoon and set aside. Add the whole chicken to the pot, breast down. Cook just until the skin turns lightly golden, 2 to 3 minutes. Turn the chicken onto its back and then onto each side, cooking until lightly golden with each turn. Remove to a platter and set aside.

Reduce the heat to medium, sprinkle in the ginger and cumin, and stir, letting the spices brown for a minute or two. Gradually add the water to the pot, stirring to scrape up any bits clinging to the bottom. Stir in the pepper, saffron, salt, and cinnamon, then add the bunches of cilantro and parsley and the sautéed onions and garlic and their collected juices. Return the chicken to the pot, breast side up. Cover, reduce the heat to medium-low, and cook, basting the chicken with the juices several times during cooking, until the chicken is tender and the juices no longer run pink when a knife is inserted at the base of the thigh, 45 to 50 minutes.

Remove the chicken to a platter and cover loosely with aluminum foil to keep warm. Scoop out the cilantro and parsley bunches and discard. Increase the heat to medium-high and cook to reduce the cooking liquid to about 2 cups.

To serve, carve the chicken into serving pieces and arrange them on a platter. Pour a little of the hot reduced liquid over them, and serve the remaining in a bowl alongside. Garnish the chicken with cilantro sprigs.

SERVES 4 OR 5

Lamb and Artichoke Tajine

Artichokes are indigenous to the Mediterranean, and cooks throughout the region prepare them in numerous ways. A tajine, or Moroccan stew, is traditionally cooked in an earthenware dish with a conical lid called a tagine slaoui. Cilantro, an especially common herb in Morocco and elsewhere in North Africa, is added at the last minute to give the stew an aromatic finish.

¼ teaspoon saffron threads

I cup boiling water

2 tablespoons fresh lemon juice,
    if using fresh artichokes, plus I tablespoon

24 fresh artichokes or frozen artichoke hearts

2 tablespoons chopped garlic

2 tablespoons extra-virgin olive oil

I teaspoon ground ginger

2 pounds boneless lean lamb stew meat,
    cut into 2-inch cubes

3 cups chicken broth

½ teaspoon salt

½ teaspoon freshly ground black pepper

I large bunch plus ¼ cup fresh cilantro, chopped

I cup salt-cured black olives

In a small bowl, combine the saffron and the boiling water and let stand for 30 minutes.

Meanwhile, if using fresh artichokes, fill a large bowl with water and add the 2 tablespoons lemon juice. Working with 1 artichoke at a time, cut off the stem flush with the base and break off the tough outer leaves to reach the tender inner leaves. With a knife, trim away the tough, dark green layer where the outer leaves were attached to the base. Cut off the upper one-half to two-thirds of the artichoke and discard, then cut the artichoke in half lengthwise and remove any furry inner choke, scooping it out with the edge of a spoon. Immediately place the cut halves in the lemon water. Repeat until all the artichokes are prepared. If using frozen artichokes, set aside.

In a large Dutch oven or other heavy pot, warm the olive oil over medium-high heat. Add the garlic and sauté until translucent, 1 to 2 minutes. Add the ginger and cook, stirring, for another minute or two. Add the lamb, saffron and its liquid, broth, salt, pepper, and the chopped bunch of cilantro. Cover and simmer until the lamb is tender and can just be pulled apart with a fork, 1 to 1½ hours.

If using fresh artichoke hearts, drain and pat dry. Add the fresh or frozen artichoke hearts and the olives to the lamb and simmer, uncovered, until the artichoke hearts are tender, about 20 minutes.

Stir in the 1 tablespoon lemon juice and the ¼ cup chopped cilantro and spoon into a warmed serving bowl. Serve at once.

SERVES 6

North African Stuffed Lamb Breast

Lamb is an important meat throughout the Mediterranean, and even the lesser cuts, such as the breast and neck, are used to make delicious and festive dishes, as well as everyday ones. The stuffing made for the breast, rich with vegetables and herbs, can be used to stuff other cuts or, most traditionally, a whole spit-roasted lamb, as it is in Morocco and Tunisia. Have the butcher cut a pocket in the breast, also called lamb ribs, for the stuffing.

3 tablespoons extra-virgin olive oil

½ yellow onion, minced

4 cloves garlic, minced

½ sweet red pepper, seeded and chopped

I zucchini, chopped

I yellow crookneck squash, chopped

½ eggplant, cut into ½-inch cubes

I cup cooked long-grain white rice

¼ cup chopped fresh flat-leaf parsley

2 teaspoons fresh thyme leaves

½ teaspoon minced fresh rosemary

I teaspoon salt

¼ teaspoon cayenne pepper

½ teaspoon freshly ground black pepper

FOR THE LAMB:

I breast of lamb, about 3 pounds

I teaspoon salt

I teaspoon freshly ground black pepper

¼ teaspoon cayenne pepper

I teaspoon ground cumin

Harissa (page 116)

Preheat an oven to 350°F.

In a skillet, heat 1 tablespoon of olive oil over medium-high heat. Add the onion and sauté until translucent, 2 to 3 minutes. Add the garlic, red pepper, zucchini, and crookneck squash and sauté until the squash is just barely tender, 3 to 4 minutes.

Meanwhile, in another skillet, heat the remaining 2 tablespoons olive oil over medium heat. Add the eggplant and sauté, stirring from time to time, until soft, about 10 minutes.

In a bowl, combine the vegetables, cooked rice, parsley, thyme, rosemary, salt, black pepper, and cayenne pepper. Mix well. Taste and adjust the seasonings.

To prepare the lamb breast, rub it inside and out with the salt, pepper, cayenne, and cumin. Fill with the stuffing, but do not overstuff. Using a poultry needle and kitchen string, sew up the pocket. Place the stuffed breast on a rack in a roasting pan. Leftover stuffing can be put in a covered dish and heated in the oven 30 minutes before serving.

Roast until the lamb is tender, the meat has pulled back from the bone, and the surface is golden brown, about 1½ hours.

Remove from the oven, cover loosely with aluminum foil, and let stand for 10 minutes.

To serve, use a very sharp knife to cut between the first two ribs. Serve with a spatula or large serving spoon to keep the stuffing intact. Continue slicing and serving. Serve accompanied with the *harissa*.

SERVES 6 TO 8

Lamb Shank and Dried Fruit Braise

The dried fruits of the Mediterranean play an important role in this braise. As they cook, they slowly reduce to a sauce, mingling with the herbs. Serve with rice to soak up the juices and with cooling slices of cucumber and tomato.

1 tablespoon unsalted butter

1 tablespoon vegetable oil

2 lamb shanks, 1½ to 2 pounds total

½ yellow onion, minced

1 clove garlic, minced

1 fresh bay leaf, or ½ dried bay leaf

1 teaspoon fresh thyme

4 dried apricot halves, chopped

2 dried pear halves, chopped

2 dried peach halves, chopped

6 dried prunes, pitted and chopped

1 tablespoon all-purpose flour

1 tablespoon ground turmeric

2 dried árbol chiles or other small dried red chiles, seeded and crumbled

¾ cup dry white wine

1½ to 2 cups chicken broth

In a skillet, melt the butter with the vegetable oil over medium heat. Add the shanks and sauté, turning once, until browned, 3 to 4 minutes on each side. Remove the shanks and set aside. Discard all but 2 tablespoons of the fat from the pan. Return the skillet to medium heat and add the onion and garlic. Sauté for 1 to 2 minutes, then add the bay leaf, thyme, and all the chopped fruits. Sauté for 2 to 3 minutes, then sprinkle with the flour, turmeric and chiles. Stir for 1 to 2 minutes, then pour in the wine. Stir constantly for 2 to 3 minutes

to dislodge any bits clinging to the bottom of the pan.

Add 1½ cups of the chicken broth and return the shanks to the pan. Reduce the heat to low, cover, and simmer until the meat is tender and can be pulled away from the bone, 2 to 2½ hours. Stir occasionally while cooking, basting the shanks with the sauce. As the sauce thickens, the sugar in the fruit will cause it to stick to the pan, so you will need to stir more frequently. You may also need to add more broth to prevent scorching.

When the shanks are done, remove them from the pan and pull away or cut off the meat. Discard the bones. Skim the surface fat from the sauce. Return the meat to the sauce and cook over low heat just enough to heat the meat through, 3 to 4 minutes. Serve immediately.

SERVES 4 OR 5

✻

Veal Shanks with Lemon, Capers, and Thyme

This is a luscious dish, with lots of sauce, perfect for swabbing up with bread. Precede it with Crostini with Cranberry Beans, Roasted Garlic, and Winter Savory Spread (page 35) or perhaps Summer Vegetables in Lemon and Oregano Marinade (page 37), and accompany it with Green and Yellow Snap Bean Salad with Summer Savory (page 51).

1 tablespoon unsalted butter

4 slices veal shank, each 1 to 1½ inches thick
    and 1½ to 2 pounds total weight

2 tablespoons all-purpose flour

1 teaspoon freshly ground black pepper

1 teaspoon minced fresh thyme

½ teaspoon salt

juice of ½ lemon, plus ½ lemon,
    cut into ½-inch pieces with peel

½ cup dry white wine

1½ to 2 cups chicken broth

1 tablespoon capers, drained

1 teaspoon green peppercorns

In a skillet, melt the butter over medium heat. When it foams, add the veal and sauté, turning once, until just golden, 2 to 3 minutes total. Sprinkle the veal with the flour, pepper, thyme, and salt, then turn it and sauté for 1 minute. Add the lemon juice and the lemon pieces and cook for 1 to 2 minutes, stirring often. Pour in the white wine and stir constantly for 2 to 3 minutes to dislodge any bits clinging to the bottom of the pan. Add 1½ cups of the chicken broth, reduce the heat to low, cover, and simmer until the meat is tender and easily pierced with the tines of a fork, 1½ to 2 hours. Stir occasionally during cooking, basting the meat with the broth. You may also need to add more broth, as there should be ¾ to 1 cup of sauce when the meat is done.

Stir in the capers and green peppercorns. Remove the veal and the sauce to a warmed serving platter or bowl and serve at once.

SERVES 4

*

Classic Paella

There are numerous versions of Spain's paella, but for me the classic remains one laced with fish, shellfish, and spicy sausage. The herbs here are added in layers: the first time dried herbs are scattered across the bottom of the hot paella pan to toast a bit, and the second addition is near the end when the shellfish are added. If possible, use saffron threads, which bring a vibrant, intense taste and color to the dish. This paella is cooked outside on a grill, but it can be prepared on top of the stove as well. Any leftovers are excellent, as the flavors continue to blend and harmonize.

1½ pounds squid (see note)

2 pounds green peas, shelled

½ teaspoon salt

1 teaspoon saffron threads (about 1 big pinch)

1 cup boiling water

2 teaspoons mixed dried thyme, sage,
    and rosemary leaves

¼ cup extra-virgin olive oil

2 yellow onions, chopped

4 cloves garlic, minced

2 large red sweet peppers, seeded and
    cut lengthwise into ¼-inch-wide strips

3½ cups short-grain Spanish, Arborio,
    or other short- or medium-grain white rice

6 to 8 cups chicken broth

½-pound piece pancetta or ham,
    cut into ½-inch cubes

1 pound chorizo sausage, cut into 1-inch pieces

1 pound firm white fish fillet
    such as cod or halibut, cut into 1-inch pieces

4 large tomatoes

1 pound raw shrimp in the shell

1½ pounds mussels, scrubbed and debearded

1½ pounds clams, scrubbed

1 teaspoon fresh thyme

1 teaspoon fresh oregano

First, clean the squid: Working with 1 squid at a time, grasp the head just belove the eyes and pull gently from the body. Using a sharp knife, slice off the tentacles from the rest of the head, then squeeze out the "beak" from the base of the tentacles. Set the whole tentacles aside. Remove and discard the quill-like cartilage and entrails from the body pouch and discard. Rinse the body well, peel off the mauve-patterned skin that covers it, then cut the body cross-wise into ½-inch-wide rings. Set aside with the tentacles.

Build a medium-hot fire in a grill.

In a saucepan, combine the peas with water to cover by 2 inches. Add the salt and bring to a boil. Reduce the heat to medium and simmer until tender, 10 to 15 minutes. The length of time will depend upon the age and size of the peas. Drain and set aside.

In a small bowl, combine the saffron threads and boiling water and let stand until ready to use.

When the fire is ready, place a paella pan or other wide, shallow pan on top of the grill about 8 inches from the coals. Sprinkle in the 2 teaspoons dried herbs and stir for a few seconds. Add the olive oil, onions, and garlic and cook, stirring, until the onions are translucent, 3 to 4 minutes. Add the sweet peppers and cook for another 2 to 3 minutes until beginning to soften. Add the rice and continue to cook, stirring, until the rice glistens and has changed color slightly. Add 6 cups of the broth and the saffron with its water and bring to a boil. Add the squid, pancetta or ham, chorizo, fish, tomatoes, and peas.

(recipe continues)

Cook until most, but not all, of the liquid has been absorbed, 15 to 20 minutes. Stir from time to time and add more broth if the liquid evaporates too quickly and the rice begins to stick. Add the shrimp, mussels, and clams and let them cook, now without stirring the mixture. When the shrimp have become opaque and the shells of the clams and mussels have opened, remove the paella from the heat, sprinkle with the fresh thyme and oregano, cover lightly with foil, and let stand for 5 minutes to allow the flavors to blend.

Discard any mussels or clams that failed to open. Serve the paella hot.

SERVES 8 TO 10

NOTE: If using already-cleaned squid, you will need about 1 pound.

✤

Provençal Tart with Bacon, Ham, and Young Greens

This delectable one-dish meal is replete with flavors from the Provençal hillsides and vegetable gardens. Serve accompanied with a green salad and finish with a fruit dessert.

FOR THE PASTRY:

2 cups all-purpose flour

1 teaspoon salt

½ cup chilled unsalted butter, cut into ½-inch pieces

3 tablespoons chilled margarine, cut into ½-inch pieces

6 tablespoons ice water

FOR THE FILLING:

3 tablespoons unsalted butter

6 cups coarsely chopped mixed baby spinach,
    dandelion, escarole, radicchio, lettuces, chervil,
    and flat-leaf parsley, in any combination

1 tablespoon minced fresh chervil

1 tablespoon minced fresh flat-leaf parsley

2 cups water

½ pound thick-cut bacon, cut into ¼-inch pieces

2 whole eggs plus 2 egg yolks

¼ cup crème fraîche or sour cream

¼ cup plus 1 tablespoon grated Parmesan cheese

⅓ cup plus 2 tablespoons finely shredded Swiss cheese

¼ pound thinly sliced ham, chopped

½ teaspoon salt

½ teaspoon freshly ground black pepper

1 teaspoon water

1 tablespoon chopped mixed fresh chervil and flat-leaf
    parsley for garnish

To make the pastry, sift the flour and salt together into a bowl. Cut in the butter and margarine with a pastry blender or two knives until pea-sized balls form. Add the ice water, 1 tablespoon at a time, turning the dough with a fork and then with your fingertips. Gather the dough into a ball, wrap in plastic wrap or aluminum foil, and refrigerate for 15 minutes.

Preheat an oven to 400°F.

On a lightly floured surface, roll out the dough into a round about 9 inches in diameter and ⅛ inch thick. Drape the dough over the rolling pin and rest it over an 8-inch tart pan with a removable bottom. Unwrap the dough and press it gently into the bottom and sides of the pan. Trim the dough to within ½ inch of the edge of the pan, then fold it under the rim and press with the tips of your fingers to make a decorative edge on the crust. Line the tart shell with aluminum foil. Add a layer of pastry weights or dried beans.

Bake the crust until it barely colors, 7 to 8 minutes. Remove from the oven and lift out the weights and foil. Prick the bottom with the tines of a fork to allow steam to escape. Return the pastry shell to the oven and bake until slightly firm but not browned, 4 to 5 minutes longer. Remove from the oven and let cool completely on a rack before filling.

Reduce the oven temperature to 375°F.

To make the filling, in a large skillet, melt 2 tablespoons of the butter over medium heat. When it foams, add the mixed greens, chervil, and the minced parsley and cook, stirring, until wilted, 3 to 4 minutes. Remove from the heat and let cool.

In a small saucepan, bring the water to a boil. Add the bacon and cook for 2 minutes. Drain and pat dry.

In a bowl, beat together the whole eggs, all but 1 teaspoon of the egg yolks, the crème fraîche or sour cream, the ¼ cup Parmesan cheese, and the ⅓ cup Swiss cheese. Stir in the cooked greens and herbs, the bacon, ham, salt, and pepper.

Spoon the mixture evenly into the prepared pastry shell. Cut the remaining 1 tablespoon butter into small bits and use to dot the top. Strew the remaining 1 tablespoon Parmesan and 2 tablespoons Swiss cheese over the top. Stir the 1 teaspoon water into the reserved 1 teaspoon egg yolk and, using a pastry brush, brush the edges of the tart.

Bake until the edges are golden brown and the filling is firm and cooked through, about 35 minutes.

Remove from the oven and garnish with the chopped mixed chervil and parsley. Serve hot or at room temperature.

SERVES 4

❊

Pasta with Pressed Purple Basil Leaves and Blossoms

Herb leaves and blossoms are easily pressed between two sheets of pasta to create a design that is beautiful and delivers a bouquet of flavor. Borage blossoms with thyme leaves or with nasturtium blossoms are just two examples of the kind of colorful, flavorful combinations you can make. The pasta could be cut into various shapes, but I think the half-inch-wide ribbons are a good all-purpose choice. They can then simply be tossed with butter, olive oil, and seasonings, allowing their patterns to be evident. Served with a hearty green salad, followed by cheese and dessert, this makes a fine Mediterranean-style meal.

    2 cups all-purpose flour

    2 eggs

    3 tablespoons olive oil

    3 tablespoons water

    1 cup fresh purple basil leaves, in different sizes,
       plus 2 tablespoons chopped

    ½ cup fresh basil blossoms, plus 1 tablespoon for garnish

    ¼ cup extra-virgin olive oil

    1 tablespoon unsalted butter

    ½ teaspoon salt

    ½ teaspoon freshly ground black pepper

The pasta dough is easily made in a food processor with a metal blade and then rolled out with a manual pasta maker. Put the flour in the food processor followed by the eggs, 3 tablespoons olive oil, and the water. Process until a rough ball of dough forms. Transfer to a floured work surface and knead until elastic, 6 or 7 minutes. Wrap loosely in plastic wrap or aluminum foil and let stand at room temperature for 30 minutes.

Divide the dough into balls each about the size of a walnut. Keep them loosely covered with a damp cloth. Set the pasta machine rollers at the widest setting, dust the roller with flour and run a ball of dough through them. Reset the rollers to a medium setting and run the sheet through again. Lay the pasta sheet on a piece of floured waxed paper and arrange some of the whole basil leaves and about 2 tablespoons of the blossoms on it. Roll out a second pasta sheet in the same way. Lay the second sheet over the first sheet and gently press together to hold the leaves and blossoms in place. Run this doubled sheet through the rollers, first on a medium setting, then on the next to the narrowest. Lay the sandwiched sheets on a floured surface and cover lightly with a damp kitchen towel. Repeat until all the dough has been used. Using a very sharp knife, cut the sheets into long ½-inch-wide strips.

Bring a large saucepan three-fourths full of water to a boil. Add the salt and the pasta, stir well, and cook until al dente, 2 to 3 minutes.

Drain the pasta and place in a warmed bowl or on a serving platter. Add the extra-virgin olive oil, butter, salt, pepper, and the chopped basil, and turn gently. Garnish with the 1 tablespoon blossoms and serve immediately.

MAKES ABOUT ¾ POUND PASTA; SERVES 4 TO 6

❊

Mussel Risotto Flavored with Garlic and Thyme

This is an excellent day-after dish to make with some leftover mussels and their broth from Moules Marinière. The risotto is so good, it is worth cooking extra mussels to be sure you have some for making it.

2 cups broth from Moules Marinière (page 63)

3 to 3½ cups water

3 tablespoons unsalted butter

2 tablespoons extra-virgin olive oil

½ yellow onion, minced

I clove garlic, minced

2 cups Arborio rice

24 shelled cooked mussels from Moules Marinière

¼ cup freshly grated Parmesan cheese

I teaspoon chopped fresh thyme

salt to taste

Combine the broth and water in a saucepan, bring to a simmer, and keep at a very gentle simmer.

In another saucepan, heat 2 tablespoons of the butter with the olive oil. When they foam, add the onion and garlic and sauté until translucent, 2 to 3 minutes. Add the rice and turn it in the butter and oil until shiny, 1 to 2 minutes. Pour in one-third of the hot broth mixture and cook over medium heat, stirring almost constantly. When the broth is nearly absorbed, add about ¾ cup more liquid and continue to cook and stir until absorbed. Continue cooking, adding the liquid about ¾ cup at a time and stirring almost constantly, until the rice is almost tender and nearly all of the liquid has been absorbed, about 25 minutes total. Taste the rice. The mixture should be creamy and the rice kernels just tender but still firm in the

center. Stir in the mussels, cheese, and thyme, and cook just until the cheese has blended into the whole, the rice has become deliciously creamy, and the mussels are heated through, 2 to 3 minutes. Season with salt.

Serve immediately, spooned onto warmed plates.

SERVES 4

❊

Fettuccine with Tomatoes, Capers, and Oregano

Oregano, either fresh or dried, sets off the sweetness of the tomatoes and the acidity of the capers to make a simple and quick sauce for fettuccine, southern Italian style.

1½ teaspoons extra-virgin olive oil

I clove garlic, minced

6 tomatoes, peeled, seeded, and chopped

2 teaspoons dried oregano leaves, crumbled,
 or 2 tablespoons chopped fresh oregano

½ teaspoon salt

½ teaspoon freshly ground black pepper

I tablespoon capers, drained

¾ pound fresh fettuccine

2 tablespoons grated Parmesan cheese

In a saucepan, heat the olive oil over medium heat. Add the garlic and sauté until translucent, 1 to 2 minutes. Then add the tomatoes, the dried oregano, if using, ¼ teaspoon of the salt, and the pepper. Cook, stirring, for 2 to 3 minutes, then reduce the heat to low and simmer, uncovered, until the tomatoes have cooked down to a sauce and are no longer watery, 20 to 25 minutes. The thickness of the sauce will depend somewhat upon the type of tomatoes used. If there is still tomato "water" remaining after 30 minutes, simply pour it off.

If you are using fresh oregano, stir in all but 1 teaspoon. Cook for another few minutes, then stir in the capers.

Bring a large saucepan three-fourths full of water to a boil. Add the remaining ¼ teaspoon salt and the pasta, stir well, and cook until al dente, about 3 minutes. Drain and place in a warmed bowl or on a platter.

Pour one-fourth of the tomato sauce over the pasta and stir to moisten. Add the remaining sauce, a little at a time, stirring to mix evenly. Top with the cheese and the reserved fresh oregano, if using, and serve immediately.

SERVES 4

❇

Pappardelle with Fried Basil Leaves and Serrano Ham

Serrano, the salt-cured ham of Spain, makes a fine sweet-salty counterpoint to the crispy perfumed taste of the fried basil leaves.

1½ teaspoons salt

¾ pound dried pappardelle

olive oil for frying

36 large, unblemished fresh basil leaves, rinsed and patted thoroughly dry

2 tablespoons extra-virgin olive oil

3 ounces thinly sliced serrano ham or prosciutto, cut into slivers

¼ cup grated Parmesan cheese

½ teaspoon freshly ground black pepper

Bring a large saucepan three-fourths full of water to a boil. Add 1 teaspoon of the salt and the pappardelle, stir well, and cook until al dente, 9 to 10 minutes.

Just before the pasta is ready, pour the olive oil for frying into a skillet to a depth of ½ inch. Place over medium-high heat and heat until the oil is hot enough for a piece of basil leaf to sizzle upon contact.

When the pasta is ready, drain and place in a warmed serving bowl or platter. Add the extra-virgin olive oil, ham, cheese, the remaining ½ teaspoon salt, and the pepper and turn to coat evenly. Drop all of the basil leaves into the hot oil and fry for 20 seconds. Remove with a slotted spoon and scatter across the pasta. Serve immediately.

SERVES 4

Breads and Sweets

Many of the breads from the Mediterranean region are seasoned with herbs or the seeds of herbs, and both are sometimes added to custards, creams, ices, and other sweets. Regional home-style desserts, except those for special occasions, are often simply seasonal fruits, eaten raw, poached, or in a tart. A little mint, rosemary, or lemon thyme might be added to heighten the flavor. Elaborate concoctions of chocolate or glazed and molded cakes with fancy cream or fruit fillings are more often the purview of the bakeries that abound, even in the smallest of towns.

Again, I have been inspired by the style of Mediterranean cooking to include recipes such as Chervil Biscuits, Sage and Sausage Scones, and Double-Lemon Sugar Cookies, which are not typical of local tables, but which reflect the casual style and unique way with seasonings.

Fresh Tomato, Basil, and Black Olive Focaccia

Basil and Dried Tomato Focaccia

Slivered Onion and Thyme Focaccia

Tapenade Puff Pastry Roll

Walnut and Rosemary Flat Bread

Sage and Sausage Scones

Chervil Biscuits

Herb-Seasoned Croutons

Fennel Crackers

Sugared Borage Blossom Cupcakes

Meyer Lemon Sorbet
with Lemon Thyme

Goat Cheese Seasoned with Lavender Seeds
and Winter Savory

Grilled Peaches Topped with
Rosemary Mascarpone

Peach Gratin with Mint Sugar

Double-Lemon Sugar Cookies

Brown Sugar Pears Baked with Lavender

Apple Crumble with Lavender

Strawberry Sorbet with Rosemary

Fresh Tomato, Basil, and Black Olive Focaccia

The topping on this bread is hearty, somewhat like that of a pizza, and the focaccia can be served on its own, or it can accompany a salad or soup.

I teaspoon active dry yeast

I cup warm water

3 cups all-purpose flour, or as needed

I teaspoon salt

I tablespoon sugar

5 tablespoons extra-virgin olive oil

2 tomatoes, sliced

⅓ cup fresh basil leaves, chopped if large

¼ cup oil-cured black olives

In a small bowl, combine the yeast and warm water and stir to mix. Let stand until foamy, about 5 minutes. Put into a food processor along with the 3 cups flour, salt, sugar, and 1 tablespoon of the olive oil. Process until a ball forms, adding a little more flour if necessary.

Remove to a lightly floured work surface and knead until the dough is smooth and elastic, 6 or 7 minutes. Gather into a ball. Oil a bowl with 1 tablespoon of the olive oil, put the ball of dough in the bowl, and turn to coat with the oil. Cover the bowl with a damp kitchen towel, put in a warm place, and let the dough rise until nearly doubled in size, about 1 hour.

Punch down the dough in the bowl, cover the bowl with the towel again, and let it rise a second time until doubled in size, another 30 minutes. Meanwhile, preheat an oven to 425°F.

Turn out onto a lightly floured work surface and stretch and roll into a round about 12 inches in diameter and 1 inch thick. Then using the handle of a wooden spoon, make little dimples all over the top of the round, and brush 2 tablespoons of olive oil over the surface. Arrange the tomato slices across the surface and sprinkle them with the basil. Then dot with the olives and sprinkle with the remaining 1 tablespoon olive oil. Transfer the round to a baking sheet.

Bake until the top is lightly golden, 25 to 30 minutes. Remove from the oven and serve warm or at room temperature, cut into wedges.

SERVES 6 TO 8

❈

Basil and Dried Tomato Focaccia

Tomatoes and basil, both beloved in the Mediterranean region, bring extra flavor to this popular flat bread because the bread is full of their taste. The bread itself is a delicate orange color, flecked with bits of fresh basil and dried tomatoes.

2 packages (I scant tablespoon each) active dry yeast

1½ cups warm water

4 cups all-purpose flour

I cup coarsely chopped fresh basil

½ cup extra-virgin olive oil

12 oil-packed dried tomatoes, drained and chopped

I teaspoon fine salt

I teaspoon coarse sea salt

In a large bowl, combine the yeast and ½ cup of the warm water and stir to mix. Let stand until foamy, about

(recipe continues)

5 minutes. Add the flour, the remaining 1 cup warm water, the basil, ¼ cup of the olive oil, the tomatoes, and the fine salt. Mix well, using your hands or a wooden spoon, until a dough forms. It will be soft and sticky. Cover the bowl with a damp kitchen towel, put it in a warm place, and let the dough rise until doubles in size, about 1½ hours.

Punch down the dough and remove it from the bowl. Form it into a ball. Pour 1 tablespoon of the remaining olive oil into the bowl, then return the dough to the bowl and roll it around to cover it with the olive oil. Cover the bowl with the towel again and let it rise a second time until nearly doubled in size, 20 to 30 minutes. Meanwhile, preheat an oven to 400°F.

Using half of the remaining olive oil, heavily coat the bottom and sides of a 12-by-18-inch baking sheet. Punch down the dough, remove it from the bowl, and lay it on a heavily floured board. Stretch and pull the dough to flatten it out into a 12-by-18-inch rectangle. Using the handle of a wooden spoon, make little dimples all over the dough. Transfer the dough to the baking sheet and brush the top with the remaining olive oil. Sprinkle with the coarse salt.

Bake until the top is lightly golden, about 20 minutes. Remove from the oven and let cool for 5 to 10 minutes. Cut into squares or strips and serve.

SERVES 8 TO 10

�֎

Slivered Onion and Thyme Focaccia

As they cook atop the olive oil–doused surface of the bread, the onions brown slightly and mingle with the taste of the fresh thyme to make a tasty snack bread, one to serve with a meal or even to split horizontally for sandwiches.

1 teaspoon active dry yeast

1 cup warm water

3 cups all-purpose flour, or as needed

1 teaspoon salt

4 tablespoons extra-virgin olive oil

1 cup very thinly slivered yellow onions

¼ cup fresh thyme

1 teaspoon coarse sea salt

¼ cup finely shredded mozzarella cheese

In a small bowl, combine the yeast and warm water and stir to mix. Let stand until foamy, about 5 minutes. Put into a food processor along with flour, salt, and 1 tablespoon of the olive oil. Process until a ball forms, adding a little more flour if necessary.

Remove to a lightly floured work surface and knead until the dough is smooth and elastic, 6 or 7 minutes. Gather into a ball. Oil a bowl with 1 tablespoon of the olive oil, put the ball of dough in the bowl, and turn to coat with the oil. Cover the bowl with a damp kitchen towel, put it in a warm place, and let the dough rise until nearly doubled in size, about 1 hour.

Punch down the dough in the bowl, cover the bowl with the towel again, and let it rise a second time until doubled in size, another 30 minutes. Meanwhile, preheat an oven to 425°F.

Turn out the dough onto a lightly floured work surface and stretch and roll into a round about 12 inches in diameter and 1 inch thick. Using the handle of a wooden spoon, make little dimples all over the top of the round. Then brush the remaining 2 tablespoons olive oil over the surface. Sprinkle on the onion slivers, thyme leaves, sea salt, and cheese. Transfer the round to a baking sheet.

Bake until the top is lightly golden, 25 to 30 minutes. Remove from the oven and serve warm or at room temperature, cut into wedges.

SERVES 6 TO 8

❧

Tapenade Puff Pastry Roll

This elegant roll, filled with an olive spread and a sprinkling of fresh thyme, can serve as part of a brunch, perhaps accompanied with scrambled eggs, grilled tomatoes, and thick slices of ham or bacon. It might also be served with aperitifs.

1 sheet frozen puff pastry, about 12 by 14 inches

2 tablespoons minced fresh thyme

1½ cups Tapenade (page 116)

1 teaspoon egg yolk mixed with 1 teaspoon water

Preheat an oven to 375°F.

On a lightly floured work surface, roll out the pastry into a 14-by-20-inch rectangle no more than ¼ inch thick. Transfer to a 12-by-18-inch baking sheet, where it will overlap the edges. Sprinkle evenly with the thyme.

Spread the Tapenade lengthwise over half the dough, to within ¾ inch of the edge. Run a bead of water around the entire perimeter of the dough, then fold the uncovered side over the covered side and press the edges together to seal

securely. Brush the surface with the egg yolk mixture, being careful not to drip any onto the baking sheet, as this will bind the dough to the sheet and inhibit the rising and puffing of the dough. Using a sharp knife, make 4 diagonal, evenly spaced slits through the upper dough.

Bake until the dough has puffed and is golden brown, 25 to 30 minutes. Remove from the oven and let stand for 10 minutes before serving. To serve, cut into 1-inch-wide slices.

SERVES 12

❧

Walnut and Rosemary Flat Bread

This flavorful, light brown, pitalike bread looks almost like wheat bread because the dough is colored by ground walnuts. Rosemary and walnuts have an affinity, but you might use thyme or even sage for a different, yet still pleasing, taste. Use the bread for dipping or spread it with soft cheeses. It also is good filled with meats, cheeses, or vegetables for sandwiches.

2 packages (scant 1 tablespoon each) active dry yeast

1 teaspoon sugar

1⅓ cups warm water

3¼ cups all-purpose flour

1½ tablespoons minced fresh rosemary

3 tablespoons walnut oil or extra-virgin olive oil

1 teaspoon salt

1 cup coarsely ground walnuts

In a small bowl, combine the yeast, sugar, and warm water and stir to mix. Let stand until foamy, about 5 minutes. In a large bowl, stir together the flour and the rosemary. In a food processor, combine the yeast mixture, half of the flour mixture, 1 tablespoon of the oil, and the salt. Process 1 to 2 minutes to mix well, then add the remaining flour mixture and process until a ball forms, about 1 minute.

Remove to a lightly floured work surface and knead until the dough is smooth and elastic, 6 or 7 minutes, adding the walnuts after 4 or 5 minutes. Gather into a ball. Oil a bowl with 1 tablespoon of the oil, put the ball of dough in the bowl, and turn to coat with the oil. Cover the bowl with a damp kitchen towel, put in a warm place, and let the dough rise until nearly doubled in size, about 1 hour.

Punch down the dough in the bowl, cover with the towel again, and let rise until nearly double in size, another 15 minutes. Meanwhile, preheat an oven to 450°F.

Divide the dough into 3 equal balls. On a lightly floured work surface, roll out each ball into a round 12 inches in diameter and a scant ¼ inch thick. Place each round on a baking sheet, and brush the tops with the remaining 1 tablespoon oil. Slip 2 baking sheets onto the middle oven racks and bake until golden and cooked through, 12 to 15 minutes. Remove from oven and bake the remaining round. Serve hot, warm, or at room temperature.

MAKES THREE 12-ROUNDS; EACH ROUND
SERVES 6 TO 8

NOTE: To store, wrap the rounds in waxed paper and place in an airtight tin, where they will keep for 2 or 3 days. Alternatively, place in freezer bags and freeze for up to 6 months.

❊

Sage and Sausage Scones

These savory scones are nearly a breakfast in themselves, or they can be served along with other brunch or breakfast dishes for a special occasion. The sage accentuates the flavor of the sausage. For lunch or supper, serve them to accompany a soup or salad.

2 leeks, including ½ inch of greens,
   sliced ½ inch thick (about 1 cup)

1 teaspoon plus 1 tablespoon extra-virgin olive oil

½ pound bulk pork sausage

2½ cups all-purpose flour

2 teaspoons baking powder

½ teaspoon salt

2 tablespoons minced fresh sage

½ teaspoon freshly ground black pepper

¼ cup butter

¾ cup milk

¼ cup plain yogurt

Preheat a broiler.

In a large bowl, combine the leeks and 1 teaspoon olive oil and toss until well mixed. Spread in a single layer on a baking sheet and slip under the broiler about 3 inches from the heat source. Broil for 3 minutes, then turn and broil until the leeks have changed color slightly, about 1 to 2 minutes longer. Remove from the oven and let cool. Crumble the sausage on the same baking sheet and broil for 3 to 4 minutes, then turn and broil until very lightly browned but not crisp, 1 to 2 minutes longer. Remove from the broiler and using a slotted spoon, transfer to paper towels to drain and cool.

Preheat the oven to 425°F. Grease a clean baking sheet with the 1 tablespoon olive oil and dust it with 1 tablespoon of the flour, shaking off any excess.

With a sharp knife, mince the cooled leeks and set aside. Make sure the sausage is nicely crumbled. Sift together the remaining flour, the baking powder, and the salt into a large bowl. Stir in the sage and pepper. Cut in the butter with a pastry blender or two knives. Finish blending the mixture with your fingers, working the dough just until pea-sized balls form. Stir in the leeks and sausage, making sure they are evenly distributed. In a bowl or pitcher with a spout, mix together the milk and the yogurt until smooth. Form a well in the center of the flour mixture and pour in the milk-yogurt mixture. Mix together the liquid and the dry ingredients just until a barely sticky dough forms.

Turn out the dough onto a lightly floured work surface. Flour your hands and knead the dough for a minute or two. Using your fingertips or a rolling pin, flatten it or roll it out about 1 inch thick. Using a knife, cut the dough into 8 free-form triangles. Place them on the prepared baking sheet.

Bake until a toothpick inserted into the center of a scone comes out clean, 15 to 18 minutes. Remove from the oven and serve hot or at room temperature.

MAKES 8 SCONES

❈

Chervil Biscuits

These simple, flaky baking powder biscuits are seasoned with fresh chervil, but sage, rosemary, thyme, or sweet cicely might be used as well.

2 cups all-purpose flour

1 tablespoon baking powder

½ teaspoon salt

½ cup chilled unsalted butter

½ cup minced fresh chervil

1 cup milk

Preheat an oven to 400°F.

In a large bowl, stir together the flour, baking powder, and salt. Cut ⅓ cup of the butter into the flour with a pastry blender or two knives until pea-sized balls form. Stir in the chervil and the milk and mix well until a dough forms. The dough will be soft, but not sticky.

Using a teaspoon of the remaining butter, grease a large baking sheet. In a small saucepan, melt the remaining butter over low heat.

On a lightly floured work surface knead the dough until it softens and becomes pliable, 2 to 3 minutes. Roll or press out ½ inch thick. Using a 2-inch-round biscuit cutter or the rim of a glass, cut out the biscuits. Space them on the baking sheet about ½ inch apart and brush with the melted butter.

Bake until the palest gold, 12 to 15 minutes. Remove from the oven and serve warm.

MAKES 14 TO 16 BISCUITS

❊

Herb-Seasoned Croutons

Using fresh herbs for making croutons, as people do in the Mediterranean, will bring a zesty element to soups and salads. The cubes will be somewhat irregular in shape, but that is part of their charm.

8 slices day-old coarse country bread,
   each about 1 inch thick

¼ cup extra-virgin olive oil

2 cloves garlic, minced

½ teaspoon salt

1 tablespoon minced fresh thyme

1 tablespoon minced fresh rosemary

1 tablespoon minced fresh oregano or sweet marjoram

Without removing the crusts, cut the bread slices into 1-inch cubes. In a large skillet, heat the olive oil over medium heat. Add the garlic and sauté until translucent, 1 to 2 minutes. Add the bread cubes, reduce the heat to low, and cook slowly, turning once, until golden and crusty, 4 to 5 minutes on each side.

Sprinkle the cubes with the salt, thyme, rosemary, and oregano or marjoram. Turn a few times in the pan to coat evenly. Using a slotted spoon, transfer the croutons to paper towels to drain and cool. To store, put in a paper bag, fold the top over several times, and keep for up to 1 week.

MAKES ABOUT 32 CROUTONS, ABOUT 4 CUPS

❊

Fennel Crackers

Thin and crispy, these small anise-flavored crackers are simple to make. In Spain or Italy you might find them accompanied with a fish spread, bites of baby octopus or squid, marinated white beans, or thin slices of prosciutto.

1 package (1 scant tablespoon) active dry yeast

¼ cup warm water

¾ cup milk

1 tablespoon sugar

2 tablespoons plus 1 teaspoon unsalted butter

1 teaspoon fine salt

1 egg

1½ tablespoons fennel seeds, finely crushed

3½ to 4 cups all-purpose flour

coarse sea salt

In a large bowl, combine the yeast and warm water and stir to mix. Let stand until foamy, about 5 minutes. In a sauce-pan, heat the milk over medium heat until small bubbles appear close to the edges of the pan. Do not allow to boil. Remove from the heat and stir in the sugar, the 2 tablespoons butter, and the fine salt. Let cool to lukewarm then, using a whisk or fork, beat in the egg and fennel seeds. Add the luke-warm milk mixture to the yeast. Then add 2 cups of the flour and beat until smooth with a wooden spoon. Add another 1½ cups flour and beat until the dough has a moderately soft texture, adding more flour if necessary to achieve the correct consistency.

Turn out the dough onto a lightly floured work surface and knead until smooth and elastic, 5 or 6 minutes. Gather into a ball. Grease a bowl with the 1 teaspoon butter, put the ball of dough in the bowl, and turn to coat with the butter.

Cover the bowl with a damp kitchen towel, put in a warm place, and let the dough rise until doubled in size, about 1 hour.

Punch down the dough in the bowl, cover with the towel again, and let the dough rest for 10 minutes. Meanwhile, preheat an oven to 450°F.

Divide the dough into small balls, each about the size of a large olive. On a lightly floured work surface, roll out each ball into a paper-thin round about 2 inches in diameter. The thinner the round, the crispier the cracker. Sprinkle a baking sheet with flour and place the dough rounds on it. Sprinkle a little coarse sea salt on each round and pat it lightly into the dough. Repeat, using more baking sheets, until all the dough has been used.

Bake for 5 minutes, then turn the crackers over, and con-tinue to bake until crisp and lightly browned on both sides, about 5 minutes longer. (If air bubbles form, puncture them with the tines of a fork.) Remove and let cool somewhat before serving. Serve warm or at room temperature. To store, pack the crackers between layers of waxed paper in an airtight tin, where they will keep for 1 week.

MAKES ABOUT 70 CRACKERS

❉

Sugared Borage Blossom Cupcakes

The bright blue blossoms of borage, sugared and sparkling like crystal, make surprisingly tasty decorations for sweet desserts and treats.

FOR THE BLOSSOMS:

48 fresh borage blossoms, rinsed and
   patted thoroughly dry

½ cup granulated sugar

¼ cup gum arabic

FOR THE CUPCAKES:

2 cups sifted cake flour

1 teaspoon baking soda

½ teaspoon salt

1½ teaspoons boiling water

1 teaspoon ground cinnamon

½ teaspoon ground nutmeg

½ teaspoon ground cloves

small pinch of cayenne pepper

½ cup unsalted butter, at room temperature

1½ cups granulated sugar

2 eggs

⅔ cup buttermilk

FOR THE FROSTING:

¼ cup unsalted butter, at room temperature

2¼ cups confectioners' sugar

¼ teaspoon salt

1 teaspoon vanilla extract

2 tablespoons heavy cream

1 tablespoon light corn syrup

Preheat an oven to 375°F. Line 24 standard muffin cups with paper liners.

To prepare the blossoms, cut a large sheet of waxed paper and lay it flat on a work surface. Put the granulated sugar in a small bowl; keep a small spoon on hand. With a pair of tweezers, pick up a blossom and, using a small paintbrush, paint it all over with gum arabic. Still holding the blossom with the tweezers, spoon the sugar all over it. Set aside on the waxed paper to dry. Repeat until all the blossoms are sugared.

To make the cupcakes, sift together the sifted flour, baking soda, and salt three times into a bowl. In a small bowl, combine the boiling water, cinnamon, nutmeg, cloves, and cayenne, and mix well.

Beat the butter with a handheld electric mixer until it is fluffy. Add the granulated sugar and continue to beat until creamy. Beat in the eggs until smooth and fluffy. Stir in the spice mixture, then add the flour mixture in small portions alternately with the buttermilk, beating until smooth after each addition. Pour the batter into the paper liners, filling each liner two-thirds full.

Bake until lightly golden on top and the center of a cupcake springs back when lightly touched, 15 to 18 minutes. Remove to wire racks and let cool for 5 minutes, then turn out of the pans and place upright on the racks.

To make the frosting: In a medium-sized bowl, beat the butter until smooth. Gradually add the confectioners' sugar, beating continuously until creamy. Beat in the salt and vanilla, then gradually stir in the cream and the corn syrup until the frosting is smooth, soft, and spreadable.

Frost the cupcakes while still warm. Top each cupcake with 2 sugared blossoms. Put in a tin or a plastic box with a tightly fitting lid and store for up to 3 days.

MAKES 24 CUPCAKES

Meyer Lemon Sorbet with Lemon Thyme

Sorbets and granitas are familiar desserts in the warm Mediterranean countries, where their light, icy texture is appreciated after a meal, or even between courses. Here, the lemon thyme provides a slightly herbaceous background note to the sweet lemon taste.

I cup sugar

I cup water

6 fresh lemon thyme sprigs, each 3 inches long,
   plus small sprigs for garnish

2 cups fresh Meyer lemon juice, or
   2 cups other lemon juice plus ½ teaspoon sugar

I tablespoon fresh orange juice

I tablespoon minced fresh lemon thyme
   plus 3 tablespoons minced lemon zest

In a small saucepan, combine the sugar, water, and the 3-inch lemon thyme sprigs over medium heat. Bring to a boil, reduce the heat to medium-low, and simmer, stirring, until a thin syrup forms, about 5 minutes. Remove from the heat and let cool. Remove the sprigs and discard. Add the lemon juice and orange juice, cover, and refrigerate for at least 6 hours or for up to overnight.

When completely chilled, stir in the minced lemon thyme and 1 tablespoon of the lemon zest. Freeze in an ice cream maker according to the manufacturer's directions. Scoop into bowls and garnish with small lemon thyme sprigs and the remaining 2 tablespoons lemon zest.

MAKES ABOUT 1½ PINTS

Goat Cheese Seasoned with Lavender Seeds and Winter Savory

A lover of goat cheese, which I am, will appreciate that the peppery flavors lavender seeds and winter savory share bring an additional earthy element to the taste that goat cheese acquires as it ages. For the cheese, choose medium-fresh rounds or slightly older drier ones, although the herbs will have less chance to flavor the latter. Serve as a dessert along with slices of firm winter pears or apples.

½ teaspoon lavender seeds

½ teaspoon dried winter savory leaves

2 rounds goat cheese, 2 to 3 ounces each
   (see recipe introduction)

With your fingertips, crumble together the seeds and the winter savory, or use a mortar and pestle to grind them. The pieces of winter savory should be tiny.

Divide the mixture, as scant as it is, into 4 portions. Press a portion into the top of each cheese, then turn the cheeses over and press the remaining portions into the bottoms. Wrap in waxed paper and refrigerate the cheeses for 4 to 5 days to age them. (They can be aged longer, if desired.)

When they have aged to your satisfaction, wrap them tightly with aluminum foil and store them in the refrigerator, where they will continue to age, but at a slower rate.

SERVES 8

✤

Grilled Peaches Topped with Rosemary Mascarpone

Grilling peaches gives them a lightly caramelized flavor that goes perfectly with the earthy, resinous undertones of rosemary.

⅔ cup mascarpone cheese

⅓ cup sugar

1 tablespoon grated lemon zest

1 teaspoon minced fresh rosemary

8 peaches, peeled, halved lengthwise, and pitted

juice of 1 lemon

fresh rosemary blossoms (optional)

Build a fire in a grill.

In a bowl, combine the mascarpone, sugar, lemon zest, and rosemary and mix well. Cover and refrigerate until ready to use.

Put the peaches in a bowl with the lemon juice. Turn to coat. Cover and refrigerate until ready to cook. (They can be kept for up to 1 hour.)

When the fire is ready, place the peaches, cut sides down, on the oiled grill rack and cook until golden on the first side, 5 to 6 minutes. Turn them over and cook until they are golden on the second side and tender, 5 to 6 minutes.

Remove the peaches to individual plates. Top with the mascarpone mixture, dividing evenly, and garnish with the rosemary blossoms, if using. Serve immediately.

SERVES 8

Peach Gratin with Mint Sugar

Fruit gratins like this one have just enough batter to hold the fruit together once they are cooked, and are frequently topped with a mixture of sugar and nuts. Here, the sugar mixture includes fresh mint as well. Although the gratin is lovely served warm, you won't go amiss if you add a scoop of vanilla ice cream or a spoonful of crème anglaise.

2 tablespoons unsalted butter

2 tablespoons plus ¼ cup sugar

4 peaches, peeled, halved, and pitted

1 egg

¼ cup milk

¼ cup all-purpose flour

⅛ teaspoon salt

¼ cup crushed almonds

1 teaspoon chopped fresh mint

Preheat an oven to 425°F. Heavily grease a 9-inch pie dish, preferably glass, with the butter.

Sprinkle the 2 tablespoons sugar evenly over the bottom of the prepared pie dish. Place the halved peaches, cut side down, in the dish.

In a bowl, combine the egg, milk, flour, and salt. Mix well with a fork. Pour the batter evenly over the peaches. In a small bowl, stir together the ¼ cup sugar, the almonds, and half of the mint, then sprinkle the mixture over the peaches.

Bake until a crust has formed and the peaches are tender and baked through, about 15 minutes. Remove from the oven and sprinkle with the remaining mint. Serve hot or warm.

SERVES 6 TO 8

Double-Lemon Sugar Cookies

Lemon thyme and the juice and zest of a fresh lemon account for the flavorings here, but lemon verbena or lemon basil might replace the thyme for a slightly different, yet still satisfying, version.

1¾ cups sifted all-purpose flour

½ teaspoon baking powder

¼ teaspoon salt

⅔ cup unsalted butter, at room temperature

¾ cup sugar

1 egg

2 teaspoons minced fresh lemon thyme

2 tablespoons grated lemon zest

1 teaspoon fresh lemon juice

Preheat an oven to 400°F.

Sift together the flour, baking powder and salt onto a piece of waxed paper. In a bowl, beat together the butter and ½ cup of the sugar until light and fluffy. Beat in the egg, lemon thyme, lemon zest, and lemon juice. Then add the flour mixture in three batches, stirring each time until the dough is smooth.

On a lightly floured work surface, roll out the dough ⅛ inch thick. Using a round cookie cutter about 2 inches in diameter (or another shape) cut out the cookies. Arrange on an ungreased baking sheet, spacing them about ½ inch apart. Gather up the dough scraps, roll out, cut out additional cookies, and place on the baking sheet. Sprinkle the cookies with the remaining sugar.

Bake just until lightly browned on the bottom and pale golden on top, 6 to 8 minutes. Remove from the oven and let the cookies cool on the pan for 5 minutes, then transfer to wire racks to cool completely. Store in an airtight tin for up to 1 week.

MAKES ABOUT 36 COOKIES

❋

Brown Sugar Pears Baked with Lavender

A layer of brown sugar and butter makes a sweet syrup for the pears as they bake, and the lavender added toward the end of the cooking brings a haunting tone to the finished dish. This is the kind of dessert you find at home-cooked meals in Provence during fall and winter.

3 firm, ripe pears such as Bosc or Bartlett

¼ cup unsalted butter, cut into small pieces

½ cup firmly packed brown sugar

½ teaspoon fresh lavender blossoms

Preheat an oven to 400°F.

Peel the pears, then halve lengthwise and remove the core. Set aside.

Scatter the butter pieces over the bottom of a 9-inch square baking dish. Put the dish in the oven for about 5 minutes, or until the butter has melted. Remove and sprinkle the butter with about two-thirds of the brown sugar. Put the pears, flat side down, in the baking dish. Sprinkle them with the lavender, and then with the remaining brown sugar.

Bake until the pears are tender, 15 to 20 minutes. Remove from the oven and serve hot or warm.

SERVES 4

Apple Crumble with Lavender

Fall is apple time, and making an old-fashioned apple crumble spiked with the last of summer's lavender is an easy dessert for launching the season with a flourish.

I tablespoon plus ⅓ cup chilled unsalted butter

1½ pounds tart baking apples such as Granny Smith, peeled, halved, cored, and sliced lengthwise 1 inch thick

juice of 1 lemon

½ cup all-purpose flour

½ cup firmly packed brown sugar

I teaspoon ground cinnamon

½ teaspoon crumbled dried lavender

Preheat an oven to 375°F. Grease a 9-by-12-inch baking dish with the 1 tablespoon butter.

Put the apple slices into the prepared dish and pour the lemon juice evenly over them. Cut the ⅓ cup butter into small pieces and place in a bowl with the flour, sugar, cinnamon, and lavender and mix with your fingertips until crumbly. Sprinkle the flour mixture evenly over the apples.

Bake until the apples are tender when pierced with a knife and the top is browned, 30 to 35 minutes. Serve warm or at room temperature.

SERVES 6

Strawberry Sorbet with Rosemary

Minced rosemary is sometimes added to strawberries; its peppery flavor is a complement to the berries' sweetness.

2 cups sugar

I cup water

2 pints fresh strawberries

I tablespoon freshly squeezed lemon juice

2 teaspoons minced fresh rosemary

Make a sugar syrup by putting the sugar and water together in a medium-sized saucepan and bring the mixture to a boil over medium-high heat, stirring to dissolve the sugar. Remove from heat and let cool to room temperature. Hull the strawberries and purée them in a food processor or blender with the sugar syrup and lemon juice. Stir in the rosemary. Freeze in an ice cream maker according to manufacturer's directions.

MAKES ABOUT 1 QUART

Basic Herbal Recipes

This chapter includes classic and contemporary Mediterranean-style recipes for herb-based sauces; raw, cooked, and dry marinades; herb butters; dried and fresh herb mixtures; herbed oils and vinegars; and beverages. Its purpose is to provide you with a repertoire of herb options to incorporate into your own cooking.

<table>
<tr><td>

SAUCES

Basil Pesto

Cilantro Pesto

Parsley Pesto

Basil Tomato Sauce

Red Pepper Sauce

Tarragon Sauce

Herbed Yogurt Sauce

Anchovy and Caper Sauce

Tapenade

Harissa

</td><td>

HERB MARINADES

Lemon and Bay Marinade

Herbes de Provence Marinade I

Yogurt, Fennel, and Dill Marinade

Lemon and Oregano Marinade

Herbes de Provence Marinade II

Sherry and Mint Marinade

Oregano, Red Wine, and Tomato Marinade

Spicy Rub Marinade

Juniper and Sage Marinade

Coriander, Thyme, Cinnamon, and Pepper Marinade

</td></tr>
</table>

HERB BUTTERS

Nasturtium and White Pepper Butter

Sage and Mustard Butter

Double-Cinnamon Butter

Forest Butter

Chives and Chive Blossom Butter

HERB MIXTURES

Rosemary, Lavender, and Sage Mixture

Oregano and Thyme Mixture

Herbes de Provence

Forest Mixture

Fines Herbes

Bouquet Garni

Gremolata

Persillade

Thyme and Oregano Mixture

Parsley and Lovage Mixture

HERB OILS AND VINEGARS

Rosemary Oil

Herbes de Provence Oil

Basil Oil

Chile and Thyme Oil

Fennel and Coriander Oil

Nasturtium Vinegar

Raspberry-Rosemary Vinegar

Tarragon Vinegar

Fines Herbes Vinegar

HERB BEVERAGES

North African Mint Tea

Lemon Verbena Tea

Mountain Sage Tea

Rosemary-Orange Shake

Peppermint Vodka

Thyme Blossom Liqueur

Wine Cooler with Borage Blossoms

SAUCES

Sauces highly seasoned with herbs play a major role in Mediterranean cooking. They may be made of vegetables, such as roasted red peppers, olives, eggplants, or beans, or they might be constructed of fish or shellfish, such as anchovy or shrimp. These sauces almost always include olive oil and are sometimes thickened with nuts. Yogurt also serves as a sauce base, and sometimes cream is used.

The sauces are important because they provide intense flavor for otherwise simple pasta, polenta, and rice dishes. They can be spooned over meats, stirred into soups and stews, or spread on toasts that have been drizzled with olive oil. Herbed sauces play a lesser role in desserts. Even so, some sweet versions are used over plain cakes, cookies, and ice creams to give them additional flavor. Any leftover sauces can be covered and stored in the refrigerator for a few days.

Basil Pesto

Pesto made with basil is an uncooked sauce incorporating olive oil, Parmesan cheese, and either almonds or pine nuts. It can be used as a sauce for pasta, added to vegetable soups, spread on sandwiches, and served as a topping for vegetables such as potatoes, tomatoes, and beans. You might also use a spoonful in a vinaigrette or mixed with butter or a soft cheese.

1 cup fresh basil leaves

¼ cup extra-virgin olive oil, or as needed

¼ cup grated Parmesan cheese

3 tablespoons blanched almonds, or 2 tablespoons pine nuts

½ teaspoon salt

Combine the basil leaves and ¼ cup olive oil in a blender or food processor. Puree until smooth. Add the cheese, nuts, and salt and process until all the ingredients are well blended into a sauce. If the sauce seems too thick, add a little more olive oil.

MAKES ABOUT ¾ CUP

Cilantro Pesto

This cilantro pesto is spicier than the one made with basil because of the addition of hot chiles. Use it to add piquancy to soups and stews and as a spread for sandwiches.

1 cup fresh cilantro leaves

¼ cup extra-virgin olive oil, or as needed

¼ cup grated Parmesan cheese

1 jalapeño or 2 serrano chiles, seeded and coarsely chopped

3 tablespoons blanched almonds, or 2 tablespoons pine nuts

½ teaspoon salt

Combine the cilantro leaves and the ¼ cup olive oil in a blender or food processor. Puree until smooth. Add the cheese, chile(s), nuts, and salt and process until all the ingredients are well blended into a sauce. If the sauce seems too thick, add a little more olive oil.

MAKES ABOUT ¾ CUP

Parsley Pesto

Pesto made with parsley has a fresh green taste that is comple-mented by a dash of lemon juice. Use this sauce for pasta, soups, and stews, to accompany fish, as a spread for sandwiches, and with hot vegetables. Add a spoonful to a vinaigrette or to flavor a butter.

1 cup fresh flat-leaf parsley leaves

¼ cup extra-virgin olive oil

¼ cup grated Parmesan cheese

1 tablespoon fresh lemon juice

3 tablespoons blanched almonds,

  or 2 tablespoons pine nuts

½ teaspoon salt

Combine the parsley leaves and ¼ cup olive oil in a blender or food processor. Puree until smooth. Add the cheese, lemon juice, nuts, and salt and process until all the ingredients are well blended into a sauce. If the sauce seems too thick, add a little more olive oil.

MAKES ABOUT ¾ CUP

❉

Basil Tomato Sauce

Serve this all-purpose sauce over pasta, vegetables, chicken, or omelets or other egg dishes, as they do in France, Spain, or Italy. It can also be passed at the table as a sauce for beef, pork, or meaty fish such as halibut, or it can be stirred into soups and stews as a flavor element.

1 tablespoon extra-virgin olive oil

2 cloves garlic, minced

½ yellow onion, minced

6 large, very ripe tomatoes, about 3 pounds total weight,

  peeled and quartered

2 or 3 fresh thyme sprigs, or

  1 teaspoon fresh thyme leaves

¼ teaspoon salt

¼ teaspoon freshly ground black pepper

¼ cup chopped fresh basil

In a saucepan, heat the olive oil over medium heat. Add the garlic and onion and sauté until translucent, 2 to 3 minutes. Add the tomatoes and cook over medium heat, stirring often, until the tomatoes begin to break down, about 5 to 10 minutes. Add the thyme, salt, and pepper and reduce the heat to low. Simmer, uncovered, until the tomatoes have thickened into a light sauce, about 30 minutes. Some varieties of tomatoes will require longer cooking.

Once the sauce is ready, stir in the basil and remove from the heat.

MAKES ABOUT 4 CUPS

❉

Red Pepper Sauce

This smooth puree is traditionally spooned into Mediterranean Fish Soup (page 56), and can be added to other soups and stews as well. It can also be used as a sauce for filled pasta such as tortellini and ravioli, or for beef, chicken, or vegetables such as eggplant, zucchini, and pumpkin. If you want a spicier sauce, add a little cayenne pepper. This is an especially popular sauce in Spain, where peppers are an important part of the cuisine.

1 large red sweet pepper

2 ripe tomatoes, peeled and seeded

2 cloves garlic, unpeeled

2 tablespoons chopped fresh marjoram or oregano

1 slice day-old baguette

¼ cup extra-virgin olive oil

¼ teaspoon salt

¼ teaspoon freshly ground black pepper

Preheat an oven to 450°F.

Place the sweet pepper, tomatoes, and the garlic on a roasting pan and roast for about 5 minutes. Remove from the oven and put the pepper and the garlic in a sealed plastic bag for a few minutes to sweat. With your fingertips or a knife, peel away the skins and remove the seeds and ribs from the pepper. Remove the skin from the garlic and the skin and core from the tomatoes.

Place the garlic cloves, marjoram or oregano, and bread in a blender or food processor and process to grind. Add the olive oil and puree. Add the peppers, tomatoes, salt, and black pepper and puree until smooth.

MAKES ABOUT 1 CUP

❇

Tarragon Sauce

Use this sauce for poached fish or chicken.

1 tablespoon unsalted butter

2 tablespoons minced shallot

2 cups dry white wine

½ teaspoon sugar

½ teaspoon salt

½ teaspoon freshly ground black pepper

1 cup fresh tarragon leaves

In a small saucepan, melt the butter over medium heat. Add the shallot and sauté until translucent, 1 to 2 minutes. Then add the wine, sugar, salt, pepper, and tarragon. Bring to a boil and cook until reduced by half, about 5 minutes. Remove from heat. Pour into a blender and puree until smooth. Return to the saucepan to reheat before serving.

MAKES 1 CUP

❇

Herbed Yogurt Sauce

Use this sauce with cold vegetables, such as green beans, artichokes, or asparagus, as a dressing for green and mixed salads, and for fruit salads, especially those containing melon. You can also add finely chopped or minced vegetables, such as cucumber and tomatoes, to make a savory alternative to sweet yogurts. Versions of this sauce can be found in the eastern Mediterranean.

I cup plain yogurt

I tablespoon chopped fresh tarragon

I tablespoon minced fresh chives

I teaspoon chopped fresh mint

I tablespoon minced oil-packed dried tomatoes (optional)

¼ teaspoon salt

½ teaspoon freshly ground black pepper

Combine all the ingredients in a bowl and stir well. Cover and chill well before serving.

MAKES ABOUT 1½ CUPS

❋

Anchovy and Caper Sauce

Anchovies, an essential Mediterranean flavor, go surprisingly well with a number of foods, from grilled fish and beef to roasted chicken, pasta dishes, and vegetables both hot and cold. Pack the sauce, mixed with some bread crumbs and finely chopped tomatoes, in between the leaves of whole cooked artichokes, add a spoonful or two to a dish of steamed green beans, or spread over a pizza crust or focaccia and then bake.

10 anchovy fillets, preferably salt-packed (see note)

I clove garlic

I teaspoon capers, drained

¼ cup chopped fresh flat-leaf parsley

I teaspoon fresh thyme leaves

¼ teaspoon freshly ground black pepper

about ¼ cup extra-virgin olive oil

In a mortar, mash together the anchovies and garlic with a pestle to make a paste. Add the capers and mash them into the paste. Next, incorporate the parsley, thyme, and pepper, and finally add the olive oil, a little at a time, to thin the paste to the desired consistency. I like mine rather thick.

MAKES ABOUT ½ CUP

NOTE: Salt-packed whole anchovies deliver better flavor and texture than fillets packed in oil, so use them here if possible. You will need to rinse the salt from 5 whole anchovies and fillet them to arrive at the 10 fillets needed.

❋

Tapenade

I have included thyme in this recipe for tapenade, an olive paste popular in southern France, although there are many that do not call for it. I like to use the thyme because it adds an additional dimension to this intense, flavorful spread. Use it on toasts as an hors d'oeuvre, as a topping for baked potatoes or steamed vegetables such as green beans or beets, and as a condiment alongside fish.

½ pound oil-cured black olives

12 anchovy fillets, preferably salt-packed (see note, page 114)

3 tablespoons capers, drained

½ teaspoon minced fresh thyme

1 teaspoon fresh lemon juice

1 or 2 tablespoons olive oil

Press on the olives with the back of a wooden spoon to split them, then remove the pits. Put the olives, anchovies, capers, thyme, and lemon juice in a blender, and process until a paste forms. Add the olive oil, a little at a time, until the paste is smooth, but not oily. Or, if you prefer, make the paste in the traditional way, with a mortar and pestle. If not using immediately, place in a covered jar and store in the refrigerator for up to 3 months.

MAKES ABOUT 1 CUP

✤

Harissa

This fiery sauce, beloved by Tunisians, is served as a condiment at every meal, even breakfast. It is also used as a cooking ingredient.

4 dried chiles such as Anaheim, seeded

8 cloves garlic

1 teaspoon ground cumin

1 teaspoon ground turmeric

½ teaspoon dried thyme leaves

½ teaspoon salt

6 tablespoons olive oil

½ cup vegetable, beef, or chicken broth

Place the chiles in a spice grinder and grind finely. Measure out ¼ cup and reserve the remainder for another use.

In a mortar or small food processor, mash or process the garlic cloves with the ¼ cup ground chiles, the cumin, turmeric, thyme, and salt to make a thick paste. Gradually stir in the olive oil until it is fully incorporated, then gradually stir in the broth until well-combined.

MAKES ABOUT ½ CUP

✤ ✤ ✤

HERB MARINADES

Marinades are of three types: raw, cooked, and dry. The purpose of marinades is primarily to add flavor, but they may also help to tenderize, in the case of meat, and can aid in keeping food moist during cooking. They are commonly used throughout the Mediterranean, and herbs are an important element in the flavoring. Raw and cooked marinades are usually made with wine, vinegar, citrus, or yogurt and seasoned with herbs and spices. If the marinating food is to be grilled, the marinade often contains oil as well. Cooked marinades are simmered and then cooled before the meat or vegetables are added, and these are especially good for long, slow simmers of wild game or tough cuts of meat. Each recipe includes a list of suggested uses.

RAW MARINADES

Lemon and Bay Marinade

Suggested uses: grilled lamb, eggplants, zucchini, sweet peppers, artichokes, chicken.

> ¼ cup extra-virgin olive oil
> juice of 1 lemon (about ¼ cup)
> grated zest of 1 lemon
> 3 fresh bay leaves
> 1 tablespoon black peppercorns
> ½ teaspoon salt

Combine all the ingredients in a bowl and mix well.

MAKES ABOUT ½ CUP

Herbes de Provence Marinade I

Suggested uses: beef, pork, wild boar, rabbit, eggplant, zucchini, tomato, tomato sauce, pizza.

> ½ cup full-bodied red wine
> ¼ cup extra-virgin olive oil
> 2 carrots, sliced
> 1 yellow onion, sliced
> 1 tablespoon Herbes de Provence (page 125)
> 2 cloves garlic, crushed
> 1 teaspoon black peppercorns

Combine all the ingredients in a bowl and mix well.

MAKES ABOUT 1½ CUPS

Yogurt, Fennel, and Dill Marinade

Suggested uses: grilled or baked chicken, fennel bulb, pork, shrimp.

1 cup plain yogurt

1 tablespoon fennel seeds, crushed

1 teaspoon dill seeds, crushed

1 teaspoon cayenne pepper or pure ground chile

Combine all the ingredients in a bowl and mix well.

MAKES ABOUT 1 CUP

❊

Lemon and Oregano Marinade

Suggested uses: grilled or baked firm-fleshed fish, chicken, grilled or sautéed squid, artichokes, asparagus, mushrooms, sweet peppers.

½ cup fresh lemon juice

½ cup extra-virgin olive oil

2 tablespoons dried oregano leaves, crumbled

1 teaspoon freshly ground black pepper

½ teaspoon salt

Combine all the ingredients in a bowl and mix well.

MAKES ABOUT 1 CUP

❊

COOKED MARINADES

Herbes de Provence Marinade II

Suggested uses: pork or beef stews, wild boar, venison, rabbit stews.

2 tablespoons extra-virgin olive oil

1 yellow onion, sliced

6 cloves garlic, crushed and chopped

4 carrots, peeled and cut into 1-inch-thick slices

4 cups water

4 cups full-bodied red wine such as Zinfandel, Burgundy, or Cabernet Sauvignon

½ cup red wine vinegar

6 fresh thyme sprigs, each 6 inches long

3 fresh rosemary sprigs, each 6 inches long

6 fresh winter savory sprigs, each 6 inches long

4 whole cloves

2 fresh bay leaves, or 1 dried bay leaf

1 teaspoon black peppercorns

6 juniper berries

1 orange zest strip, about 4 inches long and ½ inch wide

1 teaspoon salt

In a large saucepan, heat the olive oil over medium heat. Add the onion and garlic and sauté until translucent, 2 to 3 minutes. Add the carrots and sauté until they change color slightly, 1 to 2 minutes. Add all the remaining ingredients and bring to a boil. Reduce the heat to low and simmer, uncovered, for 30 minutes.

Remove from the heat and let cool to room temperature before using.

MAKES ABOUT 4 CUPS

Sherry and Mint Marinade

Suggested uses: grilled or roasted shellfish, lamb, chicken, asparagus.

1 yellow onion, sliced

1 lemon zest strip, 2 inches long

1 orange zest strip, 2 inches long

2 cups dry sherry

4 large fresh mint sprigs

½ teaspoon salt

In a saucepan, combine all the ingredients. Place over medium-high heat and bring to a boil. Reduce the heat to low and simmer, uncovered, for about 30 minutes.

Remove from the heat and let cool to room temperature before using.

MAKES ABOUT 1 CUP

Oregano, Red Wine, and Tomato Marinade

Suggested uses: beef, rabbit, lamb, veal stews.

3 cups full-bodied red wine, such as
   Zinfandel, Burgundy, or Cabernet Sauvignon

4 tomatoes, coarsely chopped

2 yellow onions, sliced

2 celery stalks, coarsely chopped

4 fresh oregano sprigs

8 black peppercorns

1 teaspoon salt

In a saucepan, combine all the ingredients. Place over medium-high heat and bring to a boil. Reduce the heat to low and simmer, uncovered, for about 30 minutes.

Remove from heat and let cool to room temperature before using.

MAKES ABOUT 2 CUPS

DRY MARINADES

Spicy Rub Marinade

Suggested uses: grilled or roasted pork, roasted fish, chicken, turkey, potatoes, carrots, fennel.

2 dried árbol chiles, seeded

2 tablespoons coriander seeds

1 tablespoon dill seeds

1 teaspoon coarse sea salt

1 teaspoon dried rosemary leaves

½ teaspoon black peppercorns

Combine all the ingredients in a spice grinder or a mortar and grind finely. Use immediately or store in a tightly covered container.

MAKES ABOUT ¼ CUP

❈

Juniper and Sage Marinade

Suggested uses: grilled or roasted lamb, rabbit, eggplants.

20 dried sage leaves

8 juniper berries

¼ cup Dijon mustard

2 tablespoons dry white wine

Place the sage leaves and juniper berries in a spice grinder or a mortar and grind finely. Transfer to a bowl and stir in the mustard and wine to make a paste.

MAKES ABOUT ⅓ CUP

❈

Coriander, Thyme, Cinnamon, and Pepper Marinade

Suggested uses: grilled or roasted lamb, beef, pork, eggplants, potatoes, corn, zucchini.

2 tablespoons coriander seeds

1 teaspoon black peppercorns

1 piece cinnamon stick, 1 inch long

1 teaspoon dried thyme leaves

½ dried bay leaf

3 tablespoons extra-virgin olive oil

Place coriander seeds, peppercorns, cinnamon stick, thyme, and bay leaf in a spice grinder or mortar and grind finely. Transfer to a bowl and stir in the olive oil to make a paste.

MAKES ABOUT ¼ CUP

❈ ❈ ❈

HERB BUTTERS

A quick burst of flavor is delivered whenever herb butters are used. They can be as simple as butter and a single herb, or other ingredients, such as mustard or spices, might be added along with one or more herbs. Once mixed, the butters can be shaped into logs and wrapped in aluminum foil or waxed paper, chilled, and then cut into slabs for melting over vegetables, meats, and fish; for sautéing; for finishing soups or stews; or for spreading on biscuits, rolls, scones, pancakes, or other breads. The butters can also be chilled in small dishes or molds for serving.

Herb butters using green herbs will keep without flavor loss for about a week in the refrigerator. Suggested uses are included with each recipe.

Nasturtium and White Pepper Butter

Suggested uses: boiled or steamed potatoes, green beans, grilled or broiled halibut, tuna, other firm-fleshed fish.

½ cup unsalted butter, at room temperature

¼ cup chopped fresh nasturtium blossoms

I teaspoon freshly ground white pepper

In a bowl, beat together all the ingredients with a wooden spoon until well blended and fluffy. Pack into a mold or shape into a log, and cover or wrap with plastic wrap or aluminum foil. Refrigerate until ready to use.

MAKES ½ CUP

Sage and Mustard Butter

Suggested uses: baked or steamed potatoes, carrots, winter squashes.

½ cup unsalted butter, at room temperature

½ teaspoon dried sage leaves, crumbled

2 teaspoons Dijon mustard

In a bowl, beat together all ingredients with a wooden spoon until well blended and fluffy. Pack into a mold or shape into a log, and cover or wrap with plastic wrap or aluminum foil. Refrigerate until ready to use.

MAKES ½ CUP

Double-Cinnamon Butter

Suggested uses: filling for cinnamon rolls or other sweet pastries or topping for pancakes, waffles, muffins, toast.

½ cup unsalted butter, at room temperature

2 tablespoons minced fresh cinnamon basil

1 tablespoon ground cinnamon

1 tablespoon sugar

In a bowl, beat together all the ingredients with a wooden spoon until well blended and fluffy. Pack into a mold or shape into a log and cover or wrap with plastic wrap or aluminum foil. Refrigerate until ready to use.

MAKES ½ CUP

❊

Forest Butter

Suggested uses: grilled or broiled steaks, pork chops or roasts, sautéed rabbit or rabbit stew, green beans, dried beans, rice, polenta.

1 tablespoon dried mushroom slices,
  such as portobello, shiitake, or porcini

1 cup boiling water

½ cup unsalted butter, at room temperature

¼ teaspoon minced fresh rosemary

¼ teaspoon salt

¼ teaspoon freshly ground black pepper

1 tablespoon dry sherry

Put the mushrooms in a small bowl, cover with the boiling water, and let stand for 15 minutes to rehydrate. Remove the mushrooms and squeeze out the water. Mince them and place in a bowl with all the remaining ingredients. Beat with a wooden spoon until well blended and fluffy. Pack into a mold or shape into a log, and cover or wrap with plastic wrap or aluminum foil. Refrigerate until ready to use.

MAKES ½ CUP

❊

Chives and Chive Blossom Butter

Suggested uses: grilled, poached, or broiled fine-fleshed fish; baked or steamed potatoes; spinach; green beans; beets; breads; biscuits.

½ cup unsalted butter, at room temperature

2 tablespoons minced fresh chives

1 teaspoon minced fresh chive blossoms

⅛ teaspoon salt

In a bowl, beat together all the ingredients with a wooden spoon until well blended and fluffy. Pack in a mold or shape into a log, and cover or wrap with plastic wrap or aluminum foil. Refrigerate until ready to use.

MAKES ½ CUP

❊ ❊ ❊

HERB MIXTURES

Herbs, both dried and fresh, can be used in various combinations. Although some blends can be commercially purchased, it is best to make your own to be assured of the freshness and the quality of the ingredients. The yields given here can be increased or decreased, but the proportions should remain approximately the same.

Dried mixtures, which primarily rely on woody herbs, can serve as ready-to-use seasoning elements. Assemble them in advance, if you wish, but use them within six months. In contrast, fresh herb combinations must be put together just before using.

Several classic combinations for green herbs are included here, plus some woody herb mixtures that are my personal favorites. Suggested uses are included with each recipe.

DRIED HERB MIXTURES

Rosemary, Lavender, and Sage Mixture

Suggested uses: grilled or roasted pork chops or roasts, lamb chops or roasts, chicken, eggplants.

¼ cup dried rosemary leaves

1 teaspoon dried lavender blossoms

2 tablespoons dried sage leaves

Crumble the leaves and blossoms together by rubbing them between your fingertips. Store in a glass jar, tin, or paper bag in a cool, dry place.

MAKES ABOUT 6 TABLESPOONS

Oregano and Thyme Mixture

Suggested uses: vinaigrettes; steamed, boiled, or sautéed carrots; potatoes; celery root; sausage dishes; pastas; polenta; tomato sauce.

¼ cup dried oregano leaves

2 tablespoons dried thyme leaves

Crumble the leaves together by rubbing them between your fingertips. Store in a glass jar, tin, or paper bag in a cool, dry place.

MAKES ABOUT 6 TABLESPOONS

Herbes de Provence

Suggested uses: sauces, soups, stews, grilled or roasted beef, pork, chicken, lamb, eggplants, tomatoes, potatoes, zucchini.

    2 tablespoons dried winter savory leaves
    I tablespoon dried rosemary leaves
    I teaspoon dried lavender blossoms
    ¾ teaspoon dried thyme leaves
    I dried bay leaf

Crumble the leaves together by rubbing them between your fingertips. Store in a glass jar, tin, or paper bag in a cool, dry place.

MAKES ABOUT ¼ CUP

❧

Forest Mixture

Suggested uses: stews, soups, white and brown sauces for beef, pork, wild game, potatoes, carrots, parsnips.

    8 dried juniper berries
    3 tablespoons dried rosemary leaves
    3 tablespoons dried winter savory leaves
    2 tablespoons dried mushroom slices such as portobello
      or porcini

Crush the juniper berries in a mortar or spice grinder. Crumble the rosemary and winter savory leaves together by rubbing them between your fingertips. Break the mushrooms into small pieces. Combine the berries, leaves, and mushrooms and store in a glass jar, tin, or paper bag in a cool, dry place.

MAKES ABOUT ½ CUP

FRESH HERB MIXTURES

Fines Herbes

Suggested uses: omelets and other egg dishes; green salads; steamed or boiled beets; beet salad; mashed, steamed, boiled, fried, or baked potatoes or sweet potatoes.

    I teaspoon chopped fresh chervil
    I teaspoon chopped fresh tarragon
    I teaspoon chopped fresh chives

Mix together the ingredients. Add at the very end of cooking or, if an uncooked dish, just before serving.

MAKES ABOUT 1 TABLESPOON

❧

Bouquet Garni

Suggested uses: soup and stews.

    2 fresh thyme sprigs
    2 fresh flat-leaf parsley sprigs
    I fresh or dried bay leaf

Tie the herbs together with kitchen string. Add to soups or stews and remove and discard at the end of cooking.

MAKES 1 BOUQUET GARNI

❧

Gremolata

Suggested uses: beef or veal stews, broiled vegetables, gratins.

2 tablespoons chopped fresh flat-leaf parsley

1 clove garlic, minced

1 teaspoon grated lemon zest

Mix together the ingredients and scatter over the top of a dish a few minutes before the end of cooking.

MAKES ABOUT 2½ TABLESPOONS

❈

Persillade

Suggested uses: soups, stews, soft cheeses, vegetable omelets, steamed, boiled, or sautéed vegetables.

2 tablespoons chopped fresh flat-leaf parsley

1 clove garlic, minced

Mix together the ingredients and add at the very end of cooking.

MAKES ABOUT 2½ TABLESPOONS

❈

Thyme and Oregano Mixture

Suggested uses: pizza or other tomato-based sauces; roasted, grilled, or broiled meat or poultry; dried, green, and shelling beans.

2 tablespoons fresh thyme leaves, coarsely chopped

1 tablespoon fresh oregano or marjoram leaves, coarsely chopped

Mix together the ingredients and add toward the end of cooking or at the beginning to dishes that do not require long cooking.

MAKES 3 TABLESPOONS

❈

Parsley and Lovage Mixture

Suggested uses: soups, green salads, mixed vegetable salads, tuna or chicken salad.

2 tablespoons chopped fresh flat-leaf parsley

1 tablespoon chopped fresh lovage

Mix together the ingredients and add toward the end of cooking.

MAKES 3 TABLESPOONS

❈ ❈ ❈

HERB OILS AND VINEGARS

Oils and vinegars infused with herbs have a significant place in the Mediterranean pantry, where they are used before, during, and after cooking and in uncooked dishes to bring out subtle elements of flavor. Olive oil, of course, is the predominant oil in the region and is used liberally. Its flavors range from mild, golden, buttery extra-virgin oils to deep-green full-fruited ones. The lighter oils are typically chosen for the green herbs, while a full-fruited oil is used for the woody herbs such as rosemary and thyme.

Infused oils are used in marinades and salads, in baking, and to dress cooked vegetables, meats, pasta dishes, and flat breads such as pizza. Vinegars made from white wine, red wine, raspberries, and sherry are all used for herbal infusions and, like the oils, are employed to season salads and cooked vegetables. In another capacity, they are used to deglaze certain dishes and as part of the resulting sauce.

Rosemary Oil

Suggested uses: cooked vegetables, marinades, grilled vegetables, pastas, brushed on breads before or after baking.

- 1½ cup fresh rosemary sprigs
- 1½ cups extra-virgin olive oil

Crush the rosemary sprigs lightly and put them in a dry, sterilized glass jar with a lid. Pour the olive oil over them and fasten the lid. Store in a cool, dark place for several days or up to 10 days, tasting periodically to determine if the desired level of flavoring has been reached. When ready to your taste, remove the rosemary and discard or use in cooking. If desired, bottle and cork the oil in a dry, sterilized bottle. Store in a cool, dark place, where it will keep for several months.

MAKES ABOUT 1½ CUPS

Herbes de Provence Oil

Suggested uses: marinades; grilled vegetables, meats, and poultry; brushed on breads before or after baking; pastas; soups; stews.

- 4 fresh thyme sprigs
- 1 fresh or dried bay leaf
- 3 fresh winter savory sprigs
- 2 fresh sage leaves
- 1 small fresh lavender sprig
- 1½ cups extra-virgin olive oil

Crush the herb sprigs and leaves lightly and put them in a dry, sterilized glass jar with a lid. Pour the olive oil over them and fasten the lid. Store in a cool, dark place for several days or up to 10 days, tasting periodically to determine if the desired level of flavoring has been reached. When ready to your taste, remove the herbs and discard or use in cooking. If desired, bottle and cork the oil in a dry, sterilized bottle. Store in a cool, dark place, where it will keep for several months.

MAKES ABOUT 1½ CUPS

Basil Oil

Suggested uses: salad dressings, cooked vegetables, sauces, soups, stews, drizzled on poached or grilled poultry or chicken, pastas.

2 cups fresh basil leaves

I cup extra-virgin olive oil

Blanch the basil leaves by plunging them into a saucepan of boiling water for 30 seconds. Remove and rinse under cold water to stop the cooking. Pat dry between paper towels. Put in a blender with half of the oil. Puree until smooth. Put the puree and the remaining oil in a dry, sterilized glass jar with a lid and fasten the lid. Store in the refrigerator for up to 1 week. The oil will separate, and the basil puree will fall to the bottom. Simply shake it to reconstitute it. At the end of the week, if you haven't used all the flavored oil, strain it and discard the basil. If desired, bottle and cork the oil in a dry sterilized bottle. Store in the refrigerator, where it will keep up for to 2 months.

MAKES ABOUT 1 CUP

✤

Chile and Thyme Oil

Suggested uses: marinades, brushed or sprinkled on pizza or other flat breads before or after baking, cooked vegetables, grilled vegetables or poultry.

6 fresh thyme sprigs

6 black peppercorns

2 or 3 small dried red chiles

I cup extra-virgin olive oil

Crush the thyme sprigs lightly and combine them with the peppercorns and the chiles in a clean, dry glass jar with a lid. Pour the oil over them and fasten the lid. Store in a cool, dark place for several days or up to 10 days, tasting periodically to determine if the desired flavor has been reached. When ready to your taste, remove the thyme, peppercorns, and chiles and discard or use in cooking. If desired, bottle and cork the oil in a dry sterilized bottle. Store in a cool, dark place, where it will keep for several months.

MAKES ABOUT 1 CUP

✤

Fennel and Coriander Oil

Suggested uses: marinades; salad dressings; grilled vegetables, fish, or poultry; poached fish or chicken; cooked vegetables.

I tablespoon fennel seeds, crushed

I tablespoon coriander seeds, crushed

6 black peppercorns

I cup extra-virgin olive oil

Put the fennel, coriander seeds, and peppercorns in a dry, sterilized glass jar with a lid. Pour the oil over them and fasten the lid. Store in a cool, dark place for several days or up to 2 weeks, tasting periodically to determine if the desired flavor has been reached. When ready to your taste, remove the seeds and the peppercorns and discard or use in cooking. If desired, bottle and cork the oil in a dry sterilized bottle. Store in a cool, dark place, where it will keep for several months.

MAKES ABOUT 1 CUP

✤

Nasturtium Vinegar

Suggested uses: deglazing; salad dressings; cooked vegetables such as potatoes, asparagus, or spinach.

2 cups pesticide-free fresh nasturtium blossoms

1 cup white wine vinegar

Put the blossoms in a dry sterilized glass jar with a lid. Pour the vinegar over them and fasten the lid. Store in a cool, dark place. Taste after 4 days to see if the vinegar has been infused to your taste. If not, let stand for up to 10 days, then strain out and discard the blossoms. If desired, bottle and cork the vinegar in a dry sterilized bottle. Store in a cool, dark place for up to 1 year.

MAKES ABOUT 1 CUP

✢

Raspberry-Rosemary Vinegar

Suggested uses: deglazing; salad dressings; fresh fruits such as strawberries, melons, or figs.

1 cup raspberries, crushed

1 fresh rosemary sprig, 2 inches long

2 cups white wine vinegar or red wine vinegar

Put the raspberries and the rosemary in a dry, sterilized glass jar with a lid. Pour the vinegar over them and fasten the lid. Store in a cool, dark place. Taste after 4 days to see if the vinegar has been infused to your taste. If not, let stand for up to 10 days, then strain out and discard the berries and the rosemary. If desired, bottle and cork the vinegar in a dry sterilized bottle. Store in a cool, dark place for up to 1 year.

MAKES ABOUT 2 CUPS

Tarragon Vinegar

Suggested uses: deglazing; salad dressings; fish; cooked vegetables such as asparagus, potatoes, beets, or carrots.

2 cups fresh tarragon sprigs

2 cups white wine vinegar

Put the tarragon sprigs in a dry, sterilized glass jar with a lid. Pour the vinegar over them and fasten the lid. Store in a cool, dark place. Taste after 4 days to see if the vinegar has been infused to your taste. If not, let stand for up to 10 days, then strain out and discard the tarragon. If desired, bottle and cork the vinegar in a dry sterilized bottle. Store in a cool, dark place for up to 1 year.

MAKES ABOUT 2 CUPS

✢

Fines Herbes Vinegar

Suggested uses: deglazing; salad dressings; fish or chicken; cooked vegetables such as Brussels sprouts, leeks, carrots, or beets.

½ cup fresh chervil sprigs

½ cup fresh tarragon sprigs

½ cup fresh flat-leaf parsley sprigs

2 cups white wine vinegar or champagne vinegar

Put the herb sprigs in a dry, sterilized glass jar with a lid. Pour the vinegar over them and fasten the lid. Store in a cool, dark place. Taste after 4 days to see if the vinegar has been infused to your taste. If not, let stand for up to 10 days, then strain out and discard the herbs. If desired, bottle and cork the vinegar in a dry sterilized bottle. Store in a cool, dark place for up to 1 year.

MAKES ABOUT 2 CUPS

HERB BEVERAGES

Herbs are used in a number of different beverages, adding a refreshing note to cold drinks and a soothing or invigorating aspect to hot ones. Blossoms or leaves are used, sometimes both. As you increasingly learn to incorporate herbs into your cooking, you can experiment with adding them to beverages as well. Additionally, there are many herbal teas used for medicinal purposes that are not within the scope of this book.

North African Mint Tea

In North African countries, sweet mint tea is served everywhere for almost every occasion. It is a ritual rather than just a beverage. Tea is regularly offered and sipped in cafés, offices, shops, and homes. It is the beverage of both family gatherings and business meetings. Different countries have different versions, but in general green tea is brewed with a large measure of mint, either fresh or dried. In yet another version, which, since it doesn't include tea, is really an infusion, fresh or dried mint leaves are used alone, with the tea omitted entirely.

> ½ cup fresh mint leaves
>
> 2 teaspoons green tea
>
> 4 cups boiling water
>
> about 6 tablespoons honey or sugar

Rinse a teapot with hot water and put the mint and tea leaves into it. Pour in the boiling water, cover, and let steep for about 5 minutes. Pour into small glasses, using a strainer if necessary, and stir about 1 tablespoon of honey or sugar into each glass. Serve at once.

SERVES 6

Lemon Verbena Tea

This light, citrusy tea is made much like mint tea (previous recipe). An infusion of lemon verbena also can be made by simply omitting the tea. Serve accompanied with sugar, lemon, cream, and milk for each person to add as desired. I prefer mine with a little bit of milk, nothing else, but many people like their tea sugared with or without lemon, or with cream or milk.

> 1 cup fresh lemon verbena leaves or
>
> ¼ cup dried lemon verbena leaves
>
> 2 teaspoons Earl Grey tea
>
> 5 cups boiling water

Rinse a teapot with hot water and put the lemon verbena and tea into it. Pour in the boiling water, cover, and let steep for 3 to 4 minutes. Pour into cups, using a strainer if necessary, and serve at once.

SERVES 8

Mountain Sage Tea

I was served this tea as an alternative to coffee on a very cold morning at a hotel in Crete. An herbal infusion rather than a true tea, it is one of the traditional drinks of Crete and is made with the dried leaves of the sage that grows wild on the mountains. It is a deep aloe green, intensely fragrant, very potent, and warming down to the toes. This version employs common sage, Salvia officinalis, a different species from the wild plant on Crete, but it makes a fine infusion, laced with lots of sugar or honey.

1 tablespoon dried sage leaves

2½ cups boiling water

3 to 4 tablespoons sugar or honey

Rinse a teapot with hot water and put the sage leaves into it. Pour in the boiling water, cover, and let steep for 2 to 5 minutes, depending upon the strength desired. Pour into cups, using a strainer if necessary, and serve at once, accompanied with sugar or honey.

SERVES 4 TO 6

❋

Rosemary-Orange Shake

An old-fashioned milk shake is quick to make and can be given a boost of flavor with the addition of herbs. Rosemary is used here, but mint, sweet cicely, lemon verbena, or lavender would be delicious, too.

2 scoops orange sherbet

¾ cup milk

1 teaspoon minced fresh rosemary, plus 1 sprig for garnish

Chill a 12-ounce glass in the refrigerator or freezer. Put the sherbet, milk, and minced rosemary in a blender or food processor. Process just to mix. Pour into the chilled glass, garnish with the rosemary sprig, and serve at once.

SERVES 1

❋

Peppermint Vodka

Herb-flavored vodkas are not difficult to make and can be served on the rocks or as part of a mixed drink. Other interesting herbs for flavoring include lemon verbena and sweet cicely leaves or the crushed seeds of fennel or coriander.

1 pint vodka

1 cup fresh peppermint leaves

Put the vodka and the leaves in a clean, dry glass jar with a lid. Cover tightly and let stand in a cool, dark place. Taste after 4 days to see if the flavor is strong enough. If not, let stand for 3 or 4 days longer.

Strain through a funnel lined with cheesecloth into a clean, dry bottle. Cork or otherwise seal and store in a cool, dark place for up to 1 year.

MAKES ABOUT 1 PINT

❋

Thyme Blossom Liqueur

This is one of the many traditional homemade liqueurs of southern France created from combining herbs or their blossoms and the locally made eau-de-vie, a product made from the fermentation of grapes, stems, and seeds after they were pressed for wine. Here, vodka is used because the alcohol should not have a distinct flavor, but instead should take on the flavor of the herbs. Liqueur de thyme is usually made in late May when the wild thyme forms carpets of purple blooms across the hillsides and along the roads. The flavor of the finished drink is sweet, with a background taste of thyme, and its color is amber.

    1 quart vodka
    2 cups fresh thyme blossoms
    1½ cups sugar

Put the vodka in a clean, dry glass jar with a lid. Add the thyme blossoms and the sugar and stir well. Cover tightly and store it in a cool, dark place for 40 days, turning it every few days until the sugar dissolves.

At the end of 40 days, line a sieve with several layers of cheesecloth and strain the vodka through it. Discard the blossoms. Using a funnel, pour the liqueur into clean, dry bottles. Cork or otherwise seal and and store in a cool, dry place for up to 1 year.

MAKES ABOUT 1 QUART

❈

Wine Cooler with Borage Blossoms

Serve this refreshing drink late on a summer afternoon when the borage blossoms are plentiful.

    1 lemon
    1 bottle (750 ml) white wine such as Sauvignon Blanc
       or Chenin Blanc, chilled
    1 bottle (8 ounces) unflavored soda water, chilled
    ¼ cup sugar
    ice cubes
    20 fresh borage blossoms

Remove the zest from the lemon in wide strips. Cut a 1-inch-long piece of the zest into thin strips for garnish. Set aside.

In a large pitcher, stir together the wine, soda, sugar, and the large pieces of lemon zest. Put 3 or 4 ice cubes into each glass and pour in the wine mixture. Garnish each glass with 2 borage blossoms and a thin strip of the lemon zest.

SERVES 10

❈ ❈ ❈

Growing Your Own Herbs

Growing your own herbs is extremely simple. They can be started from seeds or small plants, require a minimum amount of space, and most will thrive in a location that receives direct sun for only one-half to three-quarters of each day. Almost all the culinary herbs can also be grown in containers, either outside or in a sunny indoor location. With care, many of them will flourish in pots in any part of the country on city balconies, on suburban patios, or in small backyard plots. A square foot is ample to grow a single plant of almost all of the herbs in this book, although some of the woody herbs may require pruning to stay that small. At that rate, a five-by-six-foot garden would be sufficient for the 27 herbs that are discussed, although the woody and green herbs need to be treated separately because of their differing water requirements. Herbs are also relatively free of pests and need only water, soil, good drainage, nutrients, and sun to grow. No special skills are required to produce lush, flavorful plants to use in your kitchen on a daily basis.

Herbs may be annuals, biennials, or perennials. Annuals complete their life cycle within a year. They germinate from seed, grow to size, bloom, become fertilized, produce fruits and seeds, and die. Among the most popular of the annual culinary herbs are arugula, basil, chervil, dill, borage, and mustard. Perennials are plants that live at least two years (and many considerably longer) and complete their reproductive cycle each year. Among the perennial herbs are lemon verbena, mint, rosemary, tarragon, thyme, and winter savory. Biennials, of which parsley is the most notable among the herbs, live only two years and take that full period to complete their reproductive cycle, growing the first year and reproducing the second.

The gardener's rule of thumb is that annuals usually can be readily grown from seeds because they germinate quickly. Seeds of perennials and biennials may take up to three weeks to germinate, so it is often best to purchase these herbs as seedlings or cuttings, or start them in flats inside, where their early growth can be easily supervised.

Choosing and Preparing Your Garden Space

An outside herb garden should have well-drained soil and ample sunlight. Poor drainage reduces the ability of oxygen to reach a plant's roots, which can stunt or kill it, and insufficient sunlight causes spindly plants that fail to thrive. If your only location for an herb garden isn't ideal, try anyway. Herbs are generally hardy, and some can grow adequately in poorer light. Soil drainage can be corrected to some extent by adding sand or other amendments, or by growing in potting soil in containers.

Soils are composed of particles of sand, silt, and clay plus organic matter. The relative proportions of each can tremendously alter the quality of the soil. An ideal soil, a loam, has about equal amounts of each "particle" plus a high component of organic matter, maybe 5 percent, and chemically is relatively neutral, neither too acidic nor too alkaline. Generally, acidic soils are in high rainfall areas like the Northeast and Pacific Northwest states, because the soil salts are dissolved by the precipitation and pushed below the root zone. In the arid West and Southwest, evaporation draws the dissolved salts to the soil surface and leaves them there. Adding lime corrects soils that are too acid and adding sulfur (often as gypsum) corrects soils that are too alkaline.

If your soil is a heavy clay type, work sand and organic matter such as compost and aged manure or peat moss into the top foot of the soil to amend it. Medium and light sandy soils will also benefit from the addition of organic matter, because it will increase aeration and hold moisture. With a fork or spade, turn over the soil, add any amendments, including a balanced fertilizer, break down the large clods, and make the surface smooth.

❈

Fertilizing Your Garden

Nitrogen, phosphorus, and potassium are the major elements needed for plant growth. Since the plant mines these nutrients from the soil, they must be replenished either from commercial fertilizers or decomposing organic matter. Commercial fertilizers list their contents in the percentage of each nutrient in the order nitrogen-phosphorus-potassium, so a fertilizer labeled 20-10-10 would be 20 percent nitrogen, 10 percent phosphorus, 10 percent potassium, and a balanced fertilizer, such as 20-20-20 or 10-10-10, would have equal amounts of each nutrient.

Nitrogen is the element most heavily used in plant growth, especially rapid green vegetative growth. Yellowing of the plant's older leaves usually indicates a nitrogen deficiency and signals that more should be applied. Phosphorus and potassium are necessary for a wide range of plant functions, also especially during rapid growth.

Generally, plants should be fertilized well before vigorous growth, which typically occurs in spring, so there is ample time for the fertilizer first to be dissolved into the soil solution, then to be transported into the plant. Composts and manures release their nutrients slowly over a long period of time and have much lower levels of nutrients than commercial fertilizers, so they should be used in much greater volume.

Any space will suffice to grow herbs, but in a limited space the more rapidly growing annuals may at first outcompete the perennials, so careful spacing at planting time is a consideration. Perennials should be spaced to allow for their size when fully grown, but annuals can be planted much closer and, as they grow, they can be constantly thinned by using them. It is a little easier, but certainly not mandatory, to plant annuals and perennials separately because their water requirements may vary at later stages of growth.

Sowing Seeds

Seeds should be placed in rows in small furrows about a foot apart and covered with soil to a depth about three times their diameter. Press down to firm the earth over the seeds so the soil will hold moisture against the seed coat. Very tiny seeds should be scattered on top of the soil and only pressed in lightly. If planted too deeply, they may not have the energy reserves to push seedlings up very far. Small seeds are much harder to start than large seeds because the top of the ground can dry out rapidly and pull moisture out of them, halting germination. Covering small seeds lightly with peat moss is an effective way of keeping moisture around them when they are planted shallowly. Seeds can also be scatter-planted instead of planted in rows, and then raked in, but unless the ground is relatively free of weed seed, it is more difficult to keep this type of planting well weeded. Water the seeds with a gentle spray to start germination, then keep the soil around the seeds moist for the following days until the seedlings have emerged. Don't overwater, but take care that the seeds stay moist. If seeds are moistened enough to start germination and then allowed to dry out, or if very small seedlings are allowed to dry out, it is very likely they will die.

When seedlings have four true leaves, thin them to the desired distance, then keep them weeded and watered on a regular basis.

❈

Starting Seeds Indoors

If your climate is cold or if you just want a headstart on your growing season, herb seeds can be started indoors in seedling flats about six weeks before the last local frost date.

Many perennial herb seeds are slow to germinate, sometimes taking two to three weeks, so the controlled temperature and watering they will receive indoors is much more productive. A commercial potting mix or an even mixture of peat moss and vermiculite should be adequate to fill the seedling flats. Try not to buy the cheaper mixes that are mostly wood chips, as they don't hold moisture well. Space the seeds about an inch apart and plant to a depth about three times the diameter of the seed. Tiny seeds should be just pressed into the mix. Place the flats where the temperature is 65°F to 75°F, with as much daylight as possible. Water regularly with as fine a mist as you can, so the soil mix stays moist but not soggy. When the seedlings have four true leaves, add a diluted liquid fertilizer when watering to keep them green and growing. After several weeks, when you can lift a seedling and the root ball stays attached, they are ready to transplant. If the flat is not divided into compartments, cut between the seedlings to untangle intertwined roots, making them easy to separate.

Harden-off the seedlings for a week to ten days before planting, so they cease growing and accumulate energy reserves. Do this by sharply reducing watering and putting the seedlings outside for a longer and longer period each day.

Prepare the ground, water it until moist, place the seedlings in holes slightly larger than their root balls, and pack them in with soil. Water heavily to settle the soil around the root ball. Ample moisture will be important over the next few weeks as the roots grow into the surrounding earth.

Of course, whether your herbs are in a sprawling potted collection outside your kitchen door or in a garden plot arranged in elegant geometric form, the main reason to grow herbs is to have them at hand for cooking.

ANGELICA *(Angelica archangelica)* Biennial
Angelica has very small seeds that need to be exposed to light to germinate, so they should be planted almost on top of the soil and kept moist. If possible, purchase transplants. Plant in

partial shade and leave room for the large, very attractive plant—too large for containers—that can grow to six feet tall. Keep the plant vegetative by watering and fertilizing well and trimming off any flowers before they open. Angelica can be planted in spring or fall in most climates and in spring in areas with harsh winters. Harvest the leaves and the stems.

ARUGULA (Eruca sativa) Annual

Arugula grows so rapidly and easily from seed that seeding is recommended over transplants. An added bonus is that the young, tender leaves can be snipped for delicate salads after only two weeks of growth. Arugula can be planted from early spring though early fall, and I recommend successive plantings to ensure lots of young leaves, as well as leaving a few plants to mature—they will grow to two feet tall—and bear flowers. At first, the leaves of the cultivated variety are smooth and spoon shaped. Then come leaves that are slightly indented at the base and only two or three inches long. As the plant grows, there will be deeply indented leaves up to eight inches long. The initial leaves of the wild strain exhibit deep indentation like that of the mature leaves of the cultivated, but they are far narrower and sparser.

BASIL (Ocimum basilicum) Annual

Basil seed can be sown directly into containers or into a garden space, or transplanted anytime from late spring to early summer after the ground is warm. Successive plantings every two to three weeks will ensure harvests from early summer until fall's frosts. The most common variety is sweet basil, also called Italian sweet basil, which has rather large leaves and grows to about two feet tall in warm climates. Fine leaf basil, often sold as 'Piccolo Verde' or 'Basilique Fino,' has a slightly milder, sweeter flavor than the larger leaf type. Strains of purple basil are available under several different names and are generally slightly more pungent than the green types, plus their deeply colored purple leaves and lavender blossoms are a welcome visual variation for salads and garnishes. Other varieties can have a cinnamon or lemon flavor, while Thai basil and holy basil taste distinctly of licorice.

BAY LAUREL (Laurus nobilis) Perennial

Bay is grown from rooted cuttings or seedlings and transplanted into the garden or container. These are typically purchased in two- to four-inch pots, but may be available in larger one- or five-gallon pots. Planting time is from spring through summer or again in early fall. They should be in a sunny location with at least one-half day of full sun. The soil should have good drainage, as the roots are subject to rotting in soggy, wet ground. Although bay trees are hardy to 10°F, in areas with cold winters they should be planted in a container and overwintered indoors.

BORAGE (Borago officinalis) Annual

Since it grows readily from seed, borage is best sowed directly into the garden or into containers. It also has a deep taproot, which makes successful transplanting difficult unless the seedlings and their roots are very small. Once growing, borage rapidly becomes a sprawling two-foot-high plant that can take over the garden if not kept under control by stern prunings. Few specific varieties of borage exist, but one, 'Alba,' has white blooms instead of the classic blue.

CHERVIL (Anthriscus cerefolium) Annual

Chervil thrives in cool weather, not hot, so in areas with mild winters it can be sown directly into containers or a garden space, or transplants set out, in late summer for harvest from fall through spring. In harsher climates, plant or transplant in early spring for a spring through early summer harvest. Chervil grows to about one foot high in a bushy shape. There are two main varieties, flat leaf and curly leaf. They are similar in growth pattern, with the only difference being the slightly more intense flavor of the flat leaf.

CHIVE (Allium schoenoprasum) Perennial

Chives are readily grown from seed, but since the viability of the seed decreases rapidly over a twelve-month period, all but the freshest seeds will bring disappointment with a scant crop. More often, chives are propagated by divisions, a process in which clumps of multiple roots are divided and then replanted singly. These are easily found at nurseries, especially in spring and summer. This is a popular and easy-to-grow herb. The plants can be set outdoors from early spring through fall and started indoors at any time. They are shallow rooted and rarely reach more than one foot tall, so they are especially suitable to container planting.

CILANTRO (Coriandrum sativum) Annual

Cilantro, like arugula and dill, grows so quickly from seed that transplants are unnecessary. It can be sown directly into containers or into a garden space where the plants will eventually grow to one-and-a-half to two feet tall. There are two different varieties of cilantro available that are similar in appearance and flavor, but are distinguished by the speed at which they flower and set seed. Warm weather causes cilantro to come out of its vegetative growth and start to reproduce, so a variety was selected that doesn't readily send up a seed stalk (or doesn't bolt, as it is called in the seed trade). The slower to flower, and therefore the preferred for the garden, is called 'Slo-Bolt,' and the other, more common one is simply cilantro or coriander.

DANDELION (Taraxacum officinale) Perennial

If you find seeds of either cultivated dandelion or of 'San Pasquale' or 'Catalonia' chicory, which are often sold as dandelion, do grow them. The chicories are quick to germinate from seed and are rustic and hardy plants. They can be sown from early spring through early fall, and the leaves can be cut as soon as they are a few inches high. The true cultivated dandelion, like its weed cousin, is difficult to kill. It takes longer to germinate than the chicories, but grows in sun or partial shade and can be planted in deep pots. Commercially the dandelion is usually not cut until its second year, and the leaves, which grow out twelve inches or so, are tied up to blanch the interiors. In the home garden you can cut the leaves early and treat the dandelion like an annual, or you can let it grow enough to size the root and cut from it every year. The young leaves are tender, but as they age they get coarser and more bitter.

DILL (Anethum graveolens) Biennial, usually treated as an Annual

Dill is easy to start from seed, or it can be transplanted into the garden. It should be planted in full sun in spring and thinned to twelve inches apart. Several plantings ten to fourteen days apart throughout spring and early summer will provide fresh dill until fall. The plants grow three to four feet tall with wide, open heads and lacy leaves. They will flower and set seeds readily, and when the heads start to dry they can be cut and the seeds shaken out of them. There are several varieties, all of which are suitable for the home garden. 'Dukat,' a commercial variety, is high in aromatic dill oil and has deep green leaves. 'Bouquet' is slightly shorter and more compact.

FENNEL (*Foeniculum vulgare*) Perennial

Fennel is a perennial that is often treated like an annual. Its growth habits are similar to dill, but its leaves are yellowish green. Also, like dill, the seeds can be collected from the dried flowers and used as a spice. Fennel grows readily from seed or transplants, but the plant may be a bit big for containers. Nevertheless, it is worth a try. Space seeds or seedlings about eight inches apart, because the plants need room to spread, and they may reach six feet in height. Plant fennel in spring in colder areas, but in areas with mild winter climates it can be grown year-round. Hot weather induces seed-stalk formation, flowering, and seed set.

LEMON VERBENA (*Aloysia triphylla*, also called *Lippia citriodora*) Perennial

Since lemon verbena is propagated from cuttings rather than seed, it is usually purchased potted, typically in a half-gallon size or larger. The plant, which has a beautiful arching form, will grow to about three feet in the garden, although it can reach ten feet in a favorable climate. In areas with cold winters, it is best to grow lemon verbena outside in a pot, then, in the fall, bring it inside to a protected place where it will receive at least a half day of full sun. In areas with mild winters, the shrub can be planted directly in the ground, but it will lose its leaves in late fall or winter when the weather turns cold.

LOVAGE (*Levisticum officinale*) Perennial

Lovage can be grown from seed or divisions. It should be planted in full sun, anytime in mild climates and in spring in colder climates. It will lose all its shiny, celerylike green leaves in fall, but they reappear early in spring. It is suitable for container growing, but use a large container because in the ground this plant can grow to three or four feet.

MINT (*Mentha* species) Perennial

There are hundreds of varieties of mint, some of them with distinct flavors of other foods such as apple, chocolate, and lemon, but the most frequently used culinary mint is spearmint. The seeds of all mints have a poor germination rate, so they are better grown by division and cuttings. If you have a friend or neighbor with a mint plant, you can easily start your own. Cut a six-inch piece of the plant, put it in a glass or jar partly filled with water, and it will soon grow roots. When the roots are about one-half inch long, the cutting can be planted in soil or containers in full sun or partial shade. Generally the plants are about eighteen inches tall and, since they spread by underground stems, they can be invasive over time. They should be dug up and divided every few years.

NASTURTIUM (*Tropaeolum* species) Annual

Plant in early spring after all danger of frost. The exceptionally succulent leaves and stems cannot tolerate frost. Either the dwarf or the climbing varieties can be used in containers or in the garden. Both plants ramble, but the climber can get out to six feet. The plants have round, bright green leaves on long stalks and brightly colored flowers. They require almost no care except summer watering and often reseed themselves. After planting they should be thinned to about four inches apart.

PARSLEY (*Petroselinum crispum*) Biennial

This biennial is usually treated as an annual and planted anew each spring in the garden or containers. It grows readily from seed or transplants, but the seed may take several weeks to germinate. In mild winter climates, parsley can also be planted in late summer or fall and used over the winter, but it will begin to sprout flower stalks the following summer. The seedlings should be thinned to six inches apart. Italian flat-leaf parsley, at two to three feet, is taller and more aromatic than the curly types, but their growth habits are similar. Hamburg parsley is grown for its parsniplike root, but its leaves have a lot of the characteristic flavor.

SORREL (*Rumex acetosa*) Perennial

Sorrel is commonly found growing wild in soils that have a low oxygen content like heavy, tight clays or areas that flood. 'Blonde de Lyon' is the main cultivated variety, but 'Profusion' is a new variety that stays leafy and doesn't go to seed. It is available only as a transplant. Standard varieties grow readily from seed or divisions. Sorrel should be planted in full sun in the spring in cold climates and in spring or fall in mild climates, then thinned to twelve inches apart. If the leaves are cut back before the plant flowers, several flushes of new succulent leaves will result. Sorrel can become deeply rooted, so it is not an ideal container plant. If a deep container is used, however, and the root trimmed several times a year, it is sturdy enough to survive.

SUMMER SAVORY (*Satureja hortensis*) Annual

Plant seeds or transplants in spring in full sun, then thin to twelve inches apart. Summer savory grows well in containers or even in poorer soils. It forms an open bush with many branches to about eighteen inches high. The aromatic leaves are on short, hairy stalks, and pink to purple-white flowers appear at the ends. The flowers set seeds and disperse them rapidly, so the plant will self-sow.

SWEET CICELY (*Myrrhis odorata*) Perennial

Highly aromatic, sweet cicely can grow up to three feet tall. It is quite difficult to grow from seed because the seeds need to undergo periods of freezing and thawing over a period of time in order to germinate. Seedlings or cuttings may be transplanted in spring. Leave plenty of space in the garden for this large plant, which is not suitable for containers.

TARRAGON (*Artemesia dracunculus*) Perennial

This is French tarragon, the true tarragon, and it is propagated only by cuttings. If you see tarragon seed it is for Russian tarragon, an inferior-tasting herb that is not worth growing for cooking. French tarragon should be transplanted in the spring and spaced about twelve inches apart. The plants will grow two to three feet high with bright green, shiny, intensely aromatic leaves that will get coarser and darker over the season. Tarragon does best in full sun in light soils and will adapt easily to containers. The succulent leaves can be cut back to the woody stems several times in a season.

LAVENDER (*Lavandula* species) Perennial

Lavender can be irregular from seed, and the seeds can be a little difficult, but not impossible, to start. Transplants are available from cuttings. Once started, they grow with little attention, doing well in all but the coldest climates. The plants should be spaced two to three feet apart because they can grow quite large and form a contiguous line as their branches intermingle. English lavender (*L. angustifolia*), the perfume and sachet lavender, can be three feet high and wide. 'Hidcote' and 'Munstead' are dwarf varieties that are eighteen to twenty-four inches high. The purple flowers form on twenty-four-inch spikes in the summer and, like the foliage, are full of the resinous, aromatic oil. French lavender (*L. dentata*) is not as cold tolerant as its English counterpart and is a smaller, less aromatic plant. There are several other varieties of lavender and some hybrids. All lavenders grow well in containers.

MARJORAM *(Origanum majorana)* Perennial
Marjoram can be cultivated from seed, cuttings, or root divisions. Plant in full sun or partial shade or in containers. The branches will grow to two feet high and are covered with round, greenish gray, aromatic leaves. White flower clusters appear at their tips. If left to grow, the branches will get woody, so trim them back from time to time. Marjoram is suited for all but the coldest climates.

OREGANO *(Origanum vulgare)* Perennial
Oregano grows similarly to its cousin, marjoram. It is taller, to three feet, with bigger leaves, pink flowers, and a stronger aroma. Keep it trimmed back to prevent the branches from getting woody. Oregano spreads by underground stems, so it should be dug up and divided every few years.

ROSEMARY *(Rosmarinus officinalis)* Perennial
Rosemary can be grown from seed, but the seeds are slow and irregular to germinate. Plants are readily available grown from cuttings, and these are recommended. Rosemary needs full sun or partial shade and can endure a wide range of soil types, but good drainage is essential. The plants should be spaced about two feet apart. The prostrate varieties, which do well in containers, grow about two feet tall and four feet wide, and the upright varieties can be six feet high or better. The woody branches are covered with aromatic, narrow green leaves that bear clusters of light blue flowers in the spring. Rosemary can tolerate a high degree of drought, but won't make it through the coldest winters.

SAGE *(Salvia officinalis)* Perennial
Sage can be grown in all climates, either from seed or transplants. It does best in full sun, but can survive partial shade along with poor soils if the drainage is good. It is drought tolerant, making it a good candidate for container planting. The plants are handsome, about two feet high, with aromatic two-inch-long gray-green leaves on an array of branches. Spring brings rose-colored flowers on spikes that should be cut away after bloom. The fresh leaves can be repeatedly cut to the woody stems if fertilized and watered regularly, or the plant can be ignored. The plants should be dug up and divided every few years.

THYME *(Thymus vulgaris)* Perennial
Thyme grows readily from seed or transplants and will live in any climate. It flourishes in full sun or partial shade in ground with good drainage. It is not drought tolerant and will need adequate, but not heavy, summer watering. Because it is not a large plant—only twelve inches tall at most—it is well suited to container growing. The aromatic leaves are very small on thin branches covered with tiny blossoms in the spring. Cut the wiry branches back only to the woody branches to remove the leaves. There are several varieties with different flavors, like lemon thyme or orange blossom thyme, but the common thyme has ample flavor of its own.

WINTER SAVORY *(Satureja montana)* Perennial
Winter savory plants can be transplanted into the garden anytime from early spring through midsummer. Since it is a perennial, it will lose its leaves in winter and leaf out again in spring. Winter savory can also be grown from seed, but they are small seeds, making it best to start them indoors where conditions can be closely supervised. If they are kept moist and warm, they will germinate in fourteen to twenty-one days. Look for winter savory under its common or Latin name. There are no specific varieties developed of this hardy, versatile herb. Plant in full sun or partial shade in well-drained soil or in containers.

Bibliography

Brennan, Georgeanne and Mimi Luebberman. *Little Herb Gardens.* San Francisco: Chronicle Books, 1993.

Holt, Geraldene. *Geraldene Holt's Complete Book of Herbs.* New York: Henry Holt, 1992.

Hortus Third Dictionary. New York: Macmillan, 1976.

Muenscher, Walter Conrad and Myron Arthur Rice. *Garden Spice and Wild Pot Herbs.* Ithaca, New York: Cornell University Press, 1955.

Willan, Anne. *La Varenne Practique.* London: Dorling Kindersley Limited, 1989.

Index

A

anchovies
  Anchovy and Caper Sauce, 114
  Orange Salad with Anchovies and Chives, 47–48
  salt-packed, 114
  Tapenade, 116
angelica, 15, 139, 141
Apple Crumble with Lavender, 104
artichokes
  Lamb and Artichoke Tajine, 73
  Warm Artichoke Hearts with New Potatoes and Borage Blossoms, 40
arugula, 15
  Fava Bean Salad with Winter Savory, 51–52
  growing, 141
  Orange and Arugula Salad with Chicken, 46–47

B

Bacon, Ham, and Young Greens, Provençal Tart with, 80–81
basil, 15
  Basil and Dried Tomato Focaccia, 88, 90
  Basil Oil, 130
  Basil Pesto, 110
  Basil Tomato Sauce, 111
  Caponata, 32
  Double-Cinnamon Butter, 123
  Fresh Tomato, Basil, and Black Olive Focaccia, 88
  growing, 141
  Pappardelle with Fried Basil Leaves and Serrano Ham, 85
  Pasta with Pressed Purple Basil Leaves and Blossoms, 82
  Tomato, Mozzarella, and Basil Salad, 45
bay, 23. See also Herbes de Provence
  Bouquet Garni, 125
  Coriander, Thyme, Cinnamon, and Pepper Marinade, 120
  Crostini with Cranberry Beans, Roasted Garlic, and Winter Savory Spread, 35
  Dried Fava Bean Soup with Fresh Bay and Spicy Meatballs, 52
  Grilled Cornish Hens with Thyme and Winter Savory, 70–71
  growing, 141
  Lamb Shank and Dried Fruit Braise, 76
  Lemon and Bay Marinade, 117

Lentils and Potatoes with Bay Leaves, 38–39
  Mediterranean Fish Soup, 56
  Ragout of Potatoes and Wild Fennel Greens, 42
beans
  Crostini with Cranberry Beans, Roasted Garlic, and Winter Savory Spread, 35
  Dried Fava Bean Soup with Fresh Bay and Spicy Meatballs, 52
  Fava Bean Salad with Winter Savory, 51–52
  Green and Yellow Snap Bean Salad with Summer Savory, 51
  Roasted Monkfish Tails with Fava Beans, Winter Savory, and Tomatoes, 64
  Soup of Fresh Fava Beans with Lovage and Mint Cream, 52–53
beverages
  Lemon Verbena Tea, 132
  Mountain Sage Tea, 134
  North African Mint Tea, 132
  Peppermint Vodka, 134
  Rosemary-Orange Shake, 134
  Thyme Blossom Liqueur, 135
  Wine Cooler with Borage Blossoms, 135
Biscuits, Chervil, 95
Black Olive and Squid Salad with Parsley and Mint, 43
borage, 15, 17
  growing, 141
  Sugared Borage Blossom Cupcakes, 98
  Warm Artichoke Hearts with New Potatoes and Borage Blossoms, 40
  Wine Cooler with Borage Blossoms, 135
Bouquet Garni, 125
bread
  Basil and Dried Tomato Focaccia, 88, 90
  Chervil Biscuits, 95
  Crostini with Cranberry Beans, Roasted Garlic, and Winter Savory Spread, 35
  Fennel Crackers, 96
  Fresh Tomato, Basil, and Black Olive Focaccia, 88
  Herb-Seasoned Croutons, 95
  Sage and Sausage Scones, 94
  Slivered Onion and Thyme Focaccia, 90–91
  Walnut and Rosemary Flat Bread, 93
Brown Sugar Pears Baked with Lavender, 102
bulgur
  Classic Tabbouleh, 42
Butternut Squash and Riso Soup with Fresh Oregano, 53–54

butters
  Chives and Chive Blossom Butter, 123
  Double-Cinnamon Butter, 123
  Forest Butter, 123
  Nasturtium and White Pepper Butter, 122
  Sage and Mustard Butter, 122

C

Caponata, 32
cheese
  Goat Cheese Seasoned with Lavender Seeds and Winter Savory, 99
  Grilled Peaches Topped with Rosemary Mascarpone, 101
  Provençal Tart with Bacon, Ham, and Young Greens, 80–81
  Rondelles of Fennel, Parmesan, and Button Mushrooms on Parsley, 39–40
  Slivered Onion and Thyme Focaccia, 90–91
  Tomato, Mozzarella, and Basil Salad, 45
chervil, 17. See also Fines Herbes
  Chervil Biscuits, 95
  Green Herbs and Butterhead Lettuce Salad, 48
  growing, 141–42
  Provençal Tart with Bacon, Ham, and Young Greens, 80–81
chicken
  Moroccan Spiced Chicken, 72
  Orange and Arugula Salad with Chicken, 46–47
  Roasted Chicken with Sage and Rosemary, 71
Chile and Thyme Oil, 130
Chilled Cucumber Soup with Dill and Chives, 58
Chilled Melon Soup with Cilantro, 58
Chinese parsley. See cilantro
chives, 17. See also Fines Herbes
  Chilled Cucumber Soup with Dill and Chives, 58
  Chives and Chive Blossom Butter, 123
  Fava Bean Salad with Winter Savory, 51–52
  growing, 142
  Herbed Yogurt Sauce, 114
  Minted Lamb Meatballs with Fresh Green Herbs and Yogurt, 38
  Orange Salad with Anchovies and Chives, 47–48
  Sea Bass in Herbed Saffron Broth with Riso, 67

cilantro, 17–18. *See also* coriander seeds
    Chilled Melon Soup with Cilantro, 58
    Cilantro Pesto, 110
    Classic Gazpacho, 54
    Grilled Sea Bass in White Wine and
        Coriander Sauce, 66–67
    growing, 142
    Lamb and Artichoke Tajine, 73
    Moroccan Spiced Chicken, 72
    Oven-Roasted Mussels with Spicy Cilantro
        Sauce, 66
Cinnamon Butter, Double-, 123
clams
    Clams in Herbed Broth, 63
    Classic Paella, 78, 80
Classic Gazpacho, 54
Classic Paella, 78, 80
Classic Tabbouleh, 42
Cookies, Double-Lemon Sugar, 102
coriander seeds, 17. *See also* cilantro
    Coriander, Thyme, Cinnamon, and Pepper
        Marinade, 120
    Fennel and Coriander Oil, 130
    Grilled Sea Bass in White Wine and
        Coriander Sauce, 66–67
    Spicy Rub Marinade, 120
Cornish Hens, Grilled, with Thyme and Winter
    Savory, 70–71
Couscous, Saffron and Raisin, with Fresh
    Mint, 45
Crackers, Fennel, 96
Crostini with Cranberry Beans, Roasted Garlic,
    and Winter Savory Spread, 35
Croutons, Herb-Seasoned, 95
Crumble, Apple, with Lavender, 104
cucumbers
    Chilled Cucumber Soup with Dill and
        Chives, 58
    Classic Gazpacho, 54
    Classic Tabbouleh, 42
Cupcakes, Sugared Borage Blossom, 98
cutting techniques, 26

D

dandelion, 18
    growing, 142
    Provençal Tart with Bacon, Ham, and
        Young Greens, 80–81
deep-frying, 27
desserts
    Apple Crumble with Lavender, 104
    Brown Sugar Pears Baked with
        Lavender, 102
    Double-Lemon Sugar Cookies, 102
    Goat Cheese Seasoned with Lavender
        Seeds and Winter Savory, 99

    Grilled Peaches Topped with Rosemary
        Mascarpone, 101
    Meyer Lemon Sorbet with Lemon
        Thyme, 99
    Peach Gratin with Mint Sugar, 101
    Strawberry Sorbet with Rosemary, 104
    Sugared Borage Blossom Cupcakes, 98
dill, 18
    Chilled Cucumber Soup with Dill and
        Chives, 58
    growing, 142
dill seeds, 18
    Spicy Rub Marinade, 120
    Yogurt, Fennel, and Dill Marinade, 118
Double-Cinnamon Butter, 123
Double-Lemon Sugar Cookies, 102
Dried Fava Bean Soup with Fresh Bay and Spicy
    Meatballs, 52
dried herbs
    fresh vs., 27
    green, 21
    woody, 26
Dumplings, Sage-Polenta, Eggplant and Tomato
    Soup with, 57

E

eggplant
    Caponata, 32
    Eggplant and Tomato Soup with Sage-
        Polenta Dumplings, 57
    North African Stuffed Lamb Breast, 75
    Summer Vegetables in Lemon and Oregano
        Marinade, 37
eggs
    Omelet of Fines Herbes, 32

F

fava beans
    Dried Fava Bean Soup with Fresh Bay and
        Spicy Meatballs, 52
    Fava Bean Salad with Winter Savory, 51–52
    Roasted Monkfish Tails with Fava Beans,
        Winter Savory, and Tomatoes, 64
    Soup of Fresh Fava Beans with Lovage and
        Mint Cream, 52–53
fennel, 19
    growing, 144
    Mediterranean Fish Soup, 56
    Ragout of Potatoes and Wild Fennel
        Greens, 42
    Rondelles of Fennel, Parmesan, and Button
        Mushrooms on Parsley, 39–40
    Shrimp and Scallop Skewers with
        Yogurt–Wild Fennel Marinade, 34

fennel seeds, 19
    Fennel and Coriander Oil, 130
    Fennel Crackers, 96
    Shrimp and Scallop Skewers with
        Yogurt–Wild Fennel Marinade, 34
    Yogurt, Fennel, and Dill Marinade, 118
fertilizing, 138
Fettuccine with Tomatoes, Capers, and Oregano,
    84–85
Fines Herbes, 125
    Fines Herbes Vinegar, 131
    Omelet of Fines Herbes, 32
fish
    Classic Paella, 78, 80
    Foil-Wrapped Halibut Roast Infused with
        Rosemary, 68, 70
    Grilled Sea Bass in White Wine and
        Coriander Sauce, 66–67
    Halibut Kabobs with Winter Savory and
        Lemon, 68
    Mediterranean Fish Soup, 56
    Roasted Monkfish Tails with Fava Beans,
        Winter Savory, and Tomatoes, 64
    Sea Bass in Herbed Saffron Broth with
        Riso, 67
focaccia
    Basil and Dried Tomato Focaccia, 88, 90
    Fresh Tomato, Basil, and Black Olive
        Focaccia, 88
    Slivered Onion and Thyme Focaccia, 90–91
Foil-Wrapped Halibut Roast Infused with
    Rosemary, 68, 70
Forest Butter, 123
Forest Mixture, 125
Fresh Tomato, Basil, and Black Olive
    Focaccia, 88

G

garlic chives, 17
Gazpacho, Classic, 54
Goat Cheese Seasoned with Lavender Seeds and
    Winter Savory, 99
Green and Yellow Snap Bean Salad with
    Summer Savory, 51
green herbs. *See also* growing techniques;
    individual herbs
    adding, at last minute, 26
    characteristics of, 14–15
    cutting, 26
    deep-frying, 27
    dried, 21, 27
    Green Herbs and Butterhead Lettuce
        Salad, 48
    layering flavors with, 26–27

prepared foods with, 27
toasting, 27
varieties of, 15–21
Greens, Young, Provençal Tart with Bacon, Ham, and, 80–81
Gremolata, 127
Grilled Cornish Hens with Thyme and Winter Savory, 70–71
Grilled Peaches Topped with Rosemary Mascarpone, 101
Grilled Sea Bass in White Wine and Coriander Sauce, 66–67
growing techniques, 137–47
choosing and preparing space, 138
fertilizing, 138
sowing seeds, 139
by species, 138–47
starting seeds indoors, 139

H

halibut
Foil-Wrapped Halibut Roast Infused with Rosemary, 68, 70
Halibut Kabobs with Winter Savory and Lemon, 68
ham
Classic Paella, 78, 80
Pappardelle with Fried Basil Leaves and Serrano Ham, 85
Provençal Tart with Bacon, Ham, and Young Greens, 80–81
Harissa, 116
Herbed Yogurt Sauce, 114
Herbes de Provence, 125
Herbes de Provence Marinade I, 117
Herbes de Provence Marinade II, 118
Herbes de Provence Oil, 128
Herb-Seasoned Croutons, 95

J

Juniper and Sage Marinade, 120

K

Kumquat and Pork Skewers with Dried Thyme and Lavender, 34–35

L

lamb
Lamb and Artichoke Tajine, 73
Lamb Shank and Dried Fruit Braise, 76
Minted Lamb Meatballs with Fresh Green Herbs and Yogurt, 38
North African Stuffed Lamb Breast, 75

lavender, 24. *See also* Herbes de Provence
Apple Crumble with Lavender, 104
Brown Sugar Pears Baked with Lavender, 102
Goat Cheese Seasoned with Lavender Seeds and Winter Savory, 99
growing, 145
Oranges, Walnuts, and Watercress with Lavender-Yogurt Dressing, 46
Pork and Kumquat Skewers with Dried Thyme and Lavender, 34–35
Rosemary, Lavender, and Sage Mixture, 124
layering technique, 26–27
lemons
Double-Lemon Sugar Cookies, 102
Lemon and Bay Marinade, 117
Lemon and Oregano Marinade, 118
Meyer Lemon Sorbet with Lemon Thyme, 99
Summer Vegetables in Lemon and Oregano Marinade, 37
Veal Shanks with Lemon, Capers, and Thyme, 77
lemon verbena, 19
growing, 144
Lemon Verbena Tea, 132
Lentils and Potatoes with Bay Leaves, 38–39
Lettuce Salad, Butterhead, Green Herbs and, 48
lovage, 19
growing, 144
Parsley and Lovage Mixture, 127
Salad of New Potatoes with Sweet Cicely, Lovage, and Green Peppercorns, 47
Sea Bass in Herbed Saffron Broth with Riso, 67
Soup of Fresh Fava Beans with Lovage and Mint Cream, 52–53

M

marinades
Coriander, Thyme, Cinnamon, and Pepper Marinade, 120
Herbes de Provence Marinade I, 117
Herbes de Provence Marinade II, 118
Juniper and Sage Marinade, 120
Lemon and Bay Marinade, 117
Lemon and Oregano Marinade, 118
Oregano, Red Wine, and Tomato Marinade, 119
Sherry and Mint Marinade, 119
Spicy Rub Marinade, 120
Yogurt, Fennel, and Dill Marinade, 118

marjoram, 24
growing, 147
Herb-Seasoned Croutons, 95
meatballs
Dried Fava Bean Soup with Fresh Bay and Spicy Meatballs, 52
Minted Lamb Meatballs with Fresh Green Herbs and Yogurt, 38
Mediterranean Fish Soup, 56
Melon Soup, Chilled, with Cilantro, 58
Meyer Lemon Sorbet with Lemon Thyme, 99
mint, 19–20
Black Olive and Squid Salad with Parsley and Mint, 43
Classic Tabbouleh, 42
growing, 144
Herbed Yogurt Sauce, 114
Minted Lamb Meatballs with Fresh Green Herbs and Yogurt, 38
North African Mint Tea, 132
Peach Gratin with Mint Sugar, 101
Peppermint Vodka, 134
Saffron and Raisin Couscous with Fresh Mint, 45
Sherry and Mint Marinade, 119
Soup of Fresh Fava Beans with Lovage and Mint Cream, 52–53
mixtures
Bouquet Garni, 125
Fines Herbes, 125
Forest Mixture, 125
Gremolata, 127
Herbes de Provence, 125
Oregano and Thyme Mixture, 124
Parsley and Lovage Mixture, 127
Persillade, 127
Rosemary, Lavender, and Sage Mixture, 124
Thyme and Oregano Mixture, 127
Monkfish Tails, Roasted, with Fava Beans, Winter Savory, and Tomatoes, 64
Moroccan Spiced Chicken, 72
Moules Marinière, 63
Mountain Sage Tea, 134
mushrooms
Forest Butter, 123
Forest Mixture, 125
Rondelles of Fennel, Parmesan, and Button Mushrooms on Parsley, 39–40
mussels
Classic Paella, 78, 80
Moules Marinière, 63
Mussel Risotto Flavored with Garlic and Thyme, 84

Oven-Roasted Mussels with Spicy Cilantro
    Sauce, 66

N

nasturtium, 20
    growing, 144
    Nasturtium and White Pepper Butter, 122
    Nasturtium Vinegar, 131
North African Mint Tea, 132
North African Stuffed Lamb Breast, 75

O

oils
    Basil Oil, 130
    Chile and Thyme Oil, 130
    Fennel and Coriander Oil, 130
    Herbes de Provence Oil, 128
    Rosemary Oil, 128
olives
    Black Olive and Squid Salad with Parsley
        and Mint, 43
    Caponata, 32
    Fresh Tomato, Basil, and Black Olive
        Focaccia, 88
    Lamb and Artichoke Tajine, 73
    Tapenade, 116
    Tapenade Puff Pastry Roll, 91
Omelet of Fines Herbes, 32
onions
    Slivered Onion and Thyme Focaccia, 90–91
    Summer Vegetables in Lemon and Oregano
        Marinade, 37
oranges
    Orange and Arugula Salad with Chicken,
        46–47
    Orange Salad with Anchovies and Chives,
        47–48
    Oranges, Walnuts, and Watercress with
        Lavender-Yogurt Dressing, 46
oregano, 24
    Butternut Squash and Riso Soup with Fresh
        Oregano, 53–54
    Fettuccine with Tomatoes, Capers, and
        Oregano, 84–85
    growing, 147
    Herb-Seasoned Croutons, 95
    Lemon and Oregano Marinade, 118
    Oregano and Thyme Mixture, 124
    Oregano, Red Wine, and Tomato
        Marinade, 119
    Summer Vegetables in Lemon and Oregano
        Marinade, 37
    Thyme and Oregano Mixture, 127

Oven-Roasted Mussels with Spicy Cilantro
    Sauce, 66

P

Paella, Classic, 78, 80
Pancakes, Potato-Parsley, 31
Pappardelle with Fried Basil Leaves and Serrano
    Ham, 85
parsley, 20
    Anchovy and Caper Sauce, 114
    Black Olive and Squid Salad with Parsley
        and Mint, 43
    Bouquet Garni, 125
    Clams in Herbed Broth, 63
    Classic Tabbouleh, 42
    Dried Fava Bean Soup with Fresh Bay and
        Spicy Meatballs, 52
    Fines Herbes Vinegar, 131
    Green Herbs and Butterhead Lettuce
        Salad, 48
    Gremolata, 127
    growing, 144–45
    Minted Lamb Meatballs with Fresh Green
        Herbs and Yogurt, 38
    Moroccan Spiced Chicken, 72
    North African Stuffed Lamb Breast, 75
    Parsley and Lovage Mixture, 127
    Parsley Pesto, 111
    Persillade, 127
    Potato-Parsley Pancakes, 31
    Provençal Tart with Bacon, Ham, and
        Young Greens, 80–81
    Rondelles of Fennel, Parmesan, and Button
        Mushrooms on Parsley, 39–40
    Sea Bass in Herbed Saffron Broth with
        Riso, 67
pasta
    Butternut Squash and Riso Soup with Fresh
        Oregano, 53–54
    Fettuccine with Tomatoes, Capers, and
        Oregano, 84–85
    Pappardelle with Fried Basil Leaves and
        Serrano Ham, 85
    Pasta with Pressed Purple Basil Leaves and
        Blossoms, 82
    Saffron and Raisin Couscous with Fresh
        Mint, 45
    Sea Bass in Herbed Saffron Broth with
        Riso, 67
peaches
    Grilled Peaches Topped with Rosemary
        Mascarpone, 101
    Peach Gratin with Mint Sugar, 101

Pears, Brown Sugar, Baked with Lavender, 102
Peppermint Vodka, 134
peppers
    Chile and Thyme Oil, 130
    Classic Gazpacho, 54
    Red Pepper Sauce, 113
    Summer Vegetables in Lemon and Oregano
        Marinade, 37
Persillade, 127
pesto
    Basil Pesto, 110
    Cilantro Pesto, 110
    Parsley Pesto, 111
Polenta Dumplings, Sage-, Eggplant and Tomato
    Soup with, 57
pork. *See also* bacon; ham
    Classic Paella, 78, 80
    Dried Fava Bean Soup with Fresh Bay and
        Spicy Meatballs, 52
    Pork and Kumquat Skewers with Dried
        Thyme and Lavender, 34–35
    Sage and Sausage Scones, 94
potatoes
    Lentils and Potatoes with Bay Leaves, 38–39
    Mediterranean Fish Soup, 56
    Potato-Parsley Pancakes, 31
    Ragout of Potatoes and Wild Fennel
        Greens, 42
    Salad of New Potatoes with Sweet Cicely,
        Lovage, and Green Peppercorns, 47
    Warm Artichoke Hearts with New Potatoes
        and Borage Blossoms, 40
prepared foods, 27
Provençal Tart with Bacon, Ham, and Young
    Greens, 80–81
Puff Pastry Roll, Tapenade, 91

R

Ragout of Potatoes and Wild Fennel Greens, 42
Raisin and Saffron Couscous with Fresh Mint, 45
Raspberry-Rosemary Vinegar, 131
Red Pepper Sauce, 113
rice
    Classic Paella, 78, 80
    Mussel Risotto Flavored with Garlic and
        Thyme, 84
    North African Stuffed Lamb Breast, 75
Roasted Chicken with Sage and Rosemary, 71
Roasted Monkfish Tails with Fava Beans, Winter
    Savory, and Tomatoes, 64
rocket. *See* arugula
Rondelles of Fennel, Parmesan, and Button
    Mushrooms on Parsley, 39–40

rosemary, 24. *See also* Herbes de Provence
    Classic Paella, 78, 80
    Foil-Wrapped Halibut Roast Infused with
        Rosemary, 68, 70
    Forest Butter, 123
    Forest Mixture, 125
    Grilled Peaches Topped with Rosemary
        Mascarpone, 101
    growing, 147
    Herb-Seasoned Croutons, 95
    North African Stuffed Lamb Breast, 75
    Raspberry-Rosemary Vinegar, 131
    Roasted Chicken with Sage and
        Rosemary, 71
    Rosemary, Lavender, and Sage Mixture, 124
    Rosemary Oil, 128
    Rosemary-Orange Shake, 134
    Spicy Rub Marinade, 120
    Strawberry Sorbet with Rosemary, 104
    Walnut and Rosemary Flat Bread, 93

S

Saffron and Raisin Couscous with Fresh Mint, 45
sage, 24
    Classic Paella, 78, 80
    Eggplant and Tomato Soup with Sage-
        Polenta Dumplings, 57
    growing, 147
    Herbes de Provence Oil, 128
    Juniper and Sage Marinade, 120
    Mountain Sage Tea, 134
    Roasted Chicken with Sage and
        Rosemary, 71
    Rosemary, Lavender, and Sage Mixture, 124
    Sage and Mustard Butter, 122
    Sage and Sausage Scones, 94
salads
    Black Olive and Squid Salad with Parsley
        and Mint, 43
    Classic Tabbouleh, 42
    Fava Bean Salad with Winter Savory, 51–52
    Green and Yellow Snap Bean Salad with
        Summer Savory, 51
    Green Herbs and Butterhead Lettuce
        Salad, 48
    Orange and Arugula Salad with Chicken,
        46–47
    Orange Salad with Anchovies and Chives,
        47–48
    Oranges, Walnuts, and Watercress with
        Lavender-Yogurt Dressing, 46
    Rondelles of Fennel, Parmesan, and Button
        Mushrooms on Parsley, 39–40

Salad of New Potatoes with Sweet Cicely,
    Lovage, and Green Peppercorns, 47
Tomato, Mozzarella, and Basil Salad, 45
sauces
    Anchovy and Caper Sauce, 114
    Basil Pesto, 110
    Basil Tomato Sauce, 111
    Cilantro Pesto, 110
    Harissa, 116
    Herbed Yogurt Sauce, 114
    Parsley Pesto, 111
    Red Pepper Sauce, 113
    Tapenade, 116
    Tarragon Sauce, 113
sausage
    Classic Paella, 78, 80
    Dried Fava Bean Soup with Fresh Bay and
        Spicy Meatballs, 52
    Sage and Sausage Scones, 94
savory. *See* summer savory; winter savory
Scallop and Shrimp Skewers with Yogurt–Wild
    Fennel Marinade, 34
Scones, Sage and Sausage, 94
sea bass
    Grilled Sea Bass in White Wine and
        Coriander Sauce, 66–67
    Sea Bass in Herbed Saffron Broth with
        Riso, 67
seeds. *See* growing techniques
Shake, Rosemary-Orange, 134
Sherry and Mint Marinade, 119
shrimp
    Classic Paella, 78, 80
    Shrimp and Scallop Skewers with
        Yogurt–Wild Fennel Marinade, 34
Slivered Onion and Thyme Focaccia, 90–91
Sorbet, Meyer Lemon, with Lemon Thyme, 99
Sorbet, Strawberry, with Rosemary, 104
sorrel, 20
    Green Herbs and Butterhead Lettuce
        Salad, 48
    growing, 145
soups
    Butternut Squash and Riso Soup with Fresh
        Oregano, 53–54
    Chilled Cucumber Soup with Dill and
        Chives, 58
    Chilled Melon Soup with Cilantro, 58
    Classic Gazpacho, 54
    Dried Fava Bean Soup with Fresh Bay and
        Spicy Meatballs, 52
    Eggplant and Tomato Soup with Sage-
        Polenta Dumplings, 57
    Mediterranean Fish Soup, 56

Soup of Fresh Fava Beans with Lovage and
    Mint Cream, 52–53
Spicy Rub Marinade, 120
squash
    Butternut Squash and Riso Soup with Fresh
        Oregano, 53–54
    North African Stuffed Lamb Breast, 75
    Summer Vegetables in Lemon and Oregano
        Marinade, 37
squid
    Black Olive and Squid Salad with Parsley
        and Mint, 43
    Classic Paella, 78, 80
Strawberry Sorbet with Rosemary, 104
substitutions, 27
Sugared Borage Blossom Cupcakes, 98
summer savory, 21
    Green and Yellow Snap Bean Salad with
        Summer Savory, 51
    growing, 145
Summer Vegetables in Lemon and Oregano
    Marinade, 37
sweet cicely, 21
    growing, 145
    Salad of New Potatoes with Sweet Cicely,
        Lovage, and Green Peppercorns, 47
sweet marjoram. *See* marjoram

T

Tabbouleh, Classic, 42
Tapenade, 116
Tapenade Puff Pastry Roll, 91
tarragon, 21. *See also* Fines Herbes
    growing, 145
    Herbed Yogurt Sauce, 114
    Minted Lamb Meatballs with Fresh Green
        Herbs and Yogurt, 38
    Tarragon Sauce, 113
    Tarragon Vinegar, 131
Tart, Provençal, with Bacon, Ham, and Young
    Greens, 80–81
tea
    Lemon Verbena Tea, 132
    Mountain Sage Tea, 134
    North African Mint Tea, 132
thyme, 24. *See also* Herbes de Provence
    Bouquet Garni, 125
    Chile and Thyme Oil, 130
    Clams in Herbed Broth, 63
    Classic Paella, 78, 80
    Coriander, Thyme, Cinnamon, and Pepper
        Marinade, 120
    Crostini with Cranberry Beans, Roasted
        Garlic, and Winter Savory Spread, 35

Double-Lemon Sugar Cookies, 102

Eggplant and Tomato Soup with Sage-
    Polenta Dumplings, 57

Grilled Cornish Hens with Thyme and
    Winter Savory, 70–71

growing, 147

Harissa, 116

Herb-Seasoned Croutons, 95

Lamb Shank and Dried Fruit Braise, 76

Lentils and Potatoes with Bay Leaves, 38–39

Mediterranean Fish Soup, 56

Meyer Lemon Sorbet with Lemon
    Thyme, 99

Moules Marinière, 63

Mussel Risotto Flavored with Garlic and
    Thyme, 84

North African Stuffed Lamb Breast, 75

Oregano and Thyme Mixture, 124

Pork and Kumquat Skewers with Dried
    Thyme and Lavender, 34–35

Roasted Monkfish Tails with Fava Beans,
    Winter Savory, and Tomatoes, 64

Slivered Onion and Thyme Focaccia, 90–91

Tapenade, 116

Tapenade Puff Pastry Roll, 91

Thyme and Oregano Mixture, 127

Thyme Blossom Liqueur, 135

Veal Shanks with Lemon, Capers, and
    Thyme, 77

Warm Artichoke Hearts with New Potatoes
    and Borage Blossoms, 40

tomatoes

Basil and Dried Tomato Focaccia, 88, 90

Basil Tomato Sauce, 111

Caponata, 32

Classic Gazpacho, 54

Classic Tabbouleh, 42

Eggplant and Tomato Soup with Sage-
    Polenta Dumplings, 57

Fettuccine with Tomatoes, Capers, and
    Oregano, 84–85

Fresh Tomato, Basil, and Black Olive
    Focaccia, 88

Oregano, Red Wine, and Tomato
    Marinade, 119

Red Pepper Sauce, 113

Roasted Monkfish Tails with Fava Beans,
    Winter Savory, and Tomatoes, 64

Tomato, Mozzarella, and Basil Salad, 45

V

Veal Shanks with Lemon, Capers, and
    Thyme, 77

vegetables. *See also individual* vegetables

Classic Gazpacho, 54

North African Stuffed Lamb Breast, 75

Summer Vegetables in Lemon and Oregano
    Marinade, 37

vinegars

Fines Herbes Vinegar, 131

Nasturtium Vinegar, 131

Raspberry-Rosemary Vinegar, 131

Tarragon Vinegar, 131

vodka

Peppermint Vodka, 134

Thyme Blossom Liqueur, 135

W

walnuts

Oranges, Walnuts, and Watercress with
    Lavender-Yogurt Dressing, 46

Walnut and Rosemary Flat Bread, 93

Warm Artichoke Hearts with New Potatoes and
    Borage Blossoms, 40

Watercress, Oranges, and Walnuts with
    Lavender-Yogurt Dressing, 46

wild herbs, 14

wild marjoram. *See* oregano

Wine Cooler with Borage Blossoms, 135

winter savory, 26. *See also* Herbes de Provence

Crostini with Cranberry Beans, Roasted
    Garlic, and Winter Savory Spread, 35

Fava Bean Salad with Winter Savory, 51–52

Forest Mixture, 125

Goat Cheese Seasoned with Lavender Seeds
    and Winter Savory, 99

Grilled Cornish Hens with Thyme and
    Winter Savory, 70–71

growing, 147

Halibut Kabobs with Winter Savory and
    Lemon, 68

Roasted Monkfish Tails with Fava Beans,
    Winter Savory, and Tomatoes, 64

woody herbs. *See also* growing techniques;
    individual herbs

adding, at last minute, 26

characteristics of, 23

cutting, 26

deep-frying, 27

dried, 26, 27

layering flavors with, 26–27

prepared foods with, 27

toasting, 27

varieties of, 23–26

Y

yogurt

Chilled Cucumber Soup with Dill and
    Chives, 58

Herbed Yogurt Sauce, 114

Minted Lamb Meatballs with Fresh Green
    Herbs and Yogurt, 38

Oranges, Walnuts, and Watercress with
    Lavender-Yogurt Dressing, 46

Salad of New Potatoes with Sweet Cicely,
    Lovage, and Green Peppercorns, 47

Shrimp and Scallop Skewers with
    Yogurt–Wild Fennel Marinade, 34

Yogurt, Fennel, and Dill Marinade, 118

Z

zucchini. *See* squash

Table of Equivalents

The exact equivalents in the following tables have been rounded for convenience.

LIQUID/DRY MEASURES

U.S.	METRIC
¼ teaspoon	1.25 milliliters
½ teaspoon	2.5 milliliters
1 teaspoon	5 milliliters
1 tablespoon (3 teaspoons)	15 milliliters
1 fluid ounce (2 tablespoons)	30 milliliters
¼ cup	60 milliliters
⅓ cup	80 milliliters
½ cup	120 milliliters
1 cup	240 milliliters
1 pint (2 cups)	480 milliliters
1 quart (4 cups, 32 ounces)	960 milliliters
1 gallon (4 quarts)	3.84 liters
1 ounce (by weight)	28 grams
1 pound	454 grams
2.2 pounds	1 kilogram

LENGTH

U.S.	METRIC
⅛ inch	3 millimeters
¼ inch	6 millimeters
½ inch	12 millimeters
1 inch	2.5 centimeters

OVEN TEMPERATURE

FAHRENHEIT	CELSIUS	GAS
250	120	½
275	140	1
300	150	2
325	160	3
350	180	4
375	190	5
400	200	6
425	220	7
450	230	8
475	240	9
500	260	10